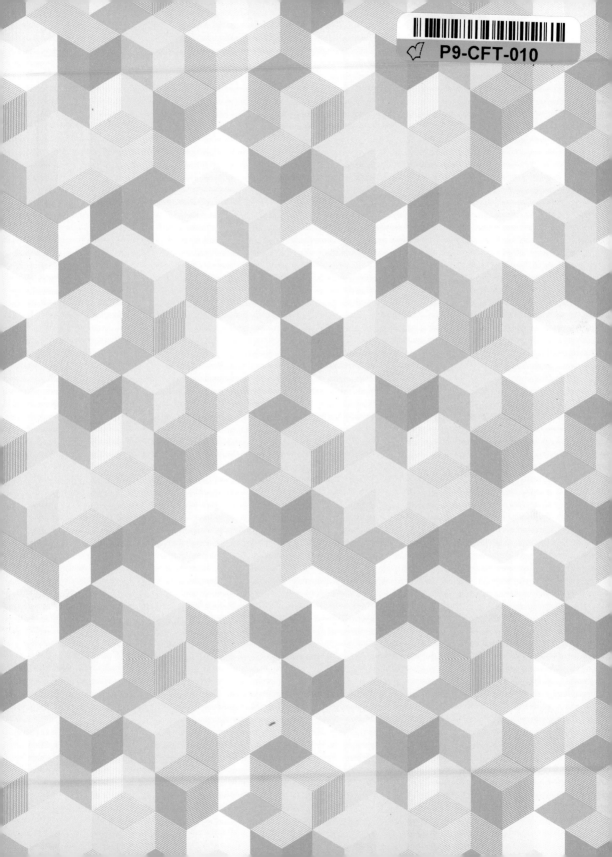

# CREATE AND CONSTRUCT:
# INCREDIBLE
## MINECRAFT® CITIES

# CREATE AND CONSTRUCT:
# INCREDIBLE
## MINECRAFT® CITIES

### KIRSTEN KEARNEY
#### WITH YAZUR STROVOZ

MITCHELL
BEAZLEY

Create and Construct: Incredible Minecraft Cities
by Kirsten Kearney

First published in Great Britain in 2015 by Mitchell Beazley,
an imprint of Octopus Publishing Group Limited,
Carmelite House
50 Victoria Embankment
London EC4Y 0DZ
www.octopusbooks.co.uk

An Hachette UK Company
www.hachette.co.uk

A CIP record for this book is available
from the British Library.
ISBN 978-1-78472-039-1

This book was conceived, designed, and produced by
Quintet Publishing Limited
114–116 Western Road
Hove, East Sussex
BN3 1DD
United Kingdom

Designer: Mark Ecob
Art Director: Michael Charles
Project Editor: Ellie Wilson
Managing Editors: Emma Bastow, Jo Turner
Publisher: Mark Searle

10 9 8 7 6

Printed in China by Toppan Leefung

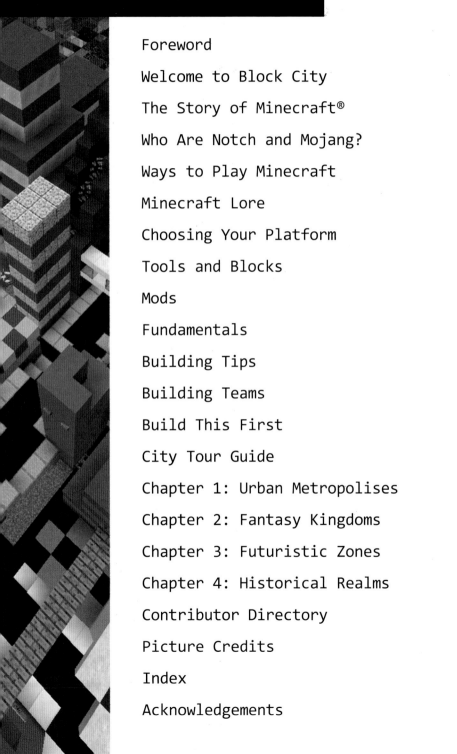

# CONTENTS

# FOREWORD

'Well, you know what has happened to Yosemite. Everybody comes, not with an ax and a box of matches, but in a trailer with a motorbike on the back and a motorboat on top and a butane stove, five aluminum folding chairs, and a transistor radio on the inside. They arrive totally encapsulated in a secondhand reality. And then they move on to Yellowstone, and it's just the same there, all trailers and transistors. They go from park to park, but they never really go anywhere; except when one of them who thinks that even the wildlife isn't real gets chewed up by a genuine, firsthand bear.'

– Ursula K. Le Guin, 'From Elfland to Poughkeepsie'

Who can forget their first day and night in the world of Minecraft®; born naked, defenceless; nervous, exhilarated; as the square sun moves across the sky?

Minecraft is, for many people, the place where they arrive with nothing but an axe and a box of matches. (OK, a pickaxe and a chest.)

It is the place where they can most be themselves. Where they can find out who they are.

Because where, now, in the real world, can we be our real selves? Where can we find out who we really are? If even Yosemite is full of tourists in RVs, 'totally encapsulated in a secondhand reality', then just look at the state of the rest of the world.

The real world is packaged. Laid out on a grid system. Owned by corporations. Covered in ads.

There are entire countries where the 'real world' has entirely vanished. The Netherlands is so engineered and artificial that more than half of it is now below sea level. Dubai is a desert Disneyland. Hong Kong, with more people living and working above the 14th floor than any other place on earth, is a city in the clouds.

We traditionally praise the real world and disparage virtual worlds; but over the years the real world has grown less real, less satisfying. Further from nature, further from the ground. Many people feel more alive, more themselves, in virtual worlds than they do in the real one. And Minecraft in particular has a simplicity and directness that the 'real' world now lacks. When Carl Jung wanted to find out who he really was,

he returned to what he loved doing as a child – playing with stones and mud. He dreamed of a house and he built it himself, over many years, and it made him whole.

But the 'real world' in which Jung built his strange and wonderful dream house no longer exists. These days, he would never get a permit to build a house he saw in a dream.

The real world has disappeared under thick layers of concrete and plastic, celebrity and terror, advertising and law.

The real world no longer exists.

And that gives us a problem.

Traditionally, you found out who you really were by going out into the real world and killing a monster, planting crops, making a cave comfortable, chopping down trees, building a hut . . .

But you can't chop down a tree in the real world, because all the trees are owned.

You can't dig a hole, because you don't have a permit.

OK, that's not totally true. I did chop down a tree this morning, in the real world, in Dublin, with an axe.

The tree broke, in a storm; a large branch came crashing down, blocking the garden. It was still partly attached to the tree by a hinge of wood. I cut it free, then cut the branch into a couple of shorter pieces, to drag it away. It was intensely pleasurable. I would like to do something like that, something real, everyday, but there aren't enough trees in our cities. If the

million people living here in Dublin did it, the four million in Berlin, the twelve million in New York, the twenty million in Shanghai . . . No, we can't cut down seven billion trees a day.

But we'd LIKE to.

We've evolved to chop things down, mine things, build things.

We've evolved to change the world.

Which made a lot of sense when there were a few thousand of us, and billions of trees, and hardly any buildings . . .

But it doesn't anymore, now that billions of us have changed the world.

Where can all that energy go now? That desire to create, and destroy, to change the world?

Well, the people in this book have arrived in a new world, 'with an axe and box of matches'. And they have tried to change the world. For the joy of it. The pleasure of creation; the pleasure of the artist; the pleasure of God.

In Minecraft®, we're in the world of Plato's essential forms: the sheep are the essence of sheep, the mountains are the essence of mountains. The human imagination fills in all the details.

Minecraft is in some ways a philosophical world in which everything has been reduced to an essence. To its simplest form.

If you want complexity, you will have to build it. But if you do build it, it will be yours – your complexity. It will be the only complexity in the world.

There are many games in which you can be Ulysses, and have adventures, fighting monsters. But very few games in which you can be Thoreau, and build a cabin by a pond, and wander, and contemplate, and dream. Build a cave, a cabin, a city . . .

Minecraft, in survival mode, does a good job of that first kind of game. But Minecraft in creative mode is that rare and wonderful second kind of game.

Most games are impatient with patience. They don't want you to be relaxed, quiet, mindful; to be absorbed in a task for hours, days, weeks, months, years.

Most games assume a hyperactivity of mind, an instability of self, a radical impatience, and so they try to amuse you, distract you, pleasure you with novelty, endlessly, forever. The result is, of course, a vision of hell.

Most games re-create, in their virtual worlds, all the stuff we play games to escape. They're full of people, things, bosses, terror, tasks, fear, status anxiety. The job of assassin is still a job. What is levelling up but the hoped-for promotion? Is our anxiety as we watch our health bar approach zero any different to our anxiety as we watch our bank account approach zero? With their guns, explosions and adrenaline-pumping music, they enhance and stylise our anxiety, our dread; they make us feel alive by convincing us we may soon be dead.

But in creative mode, Minecraft lets us feel alive by playing. Not playing at killing. Playing at playing. Because you never feel more alive than when you are playing, creating, lost in a game. Building a fort, with your friends.

With Minecraft, with creative mode, Notch said, OK, I don't know what to do. I don't know what to build. I don't know the secrets of the human heart. You're human, I trust you. Go and build the secrets of the human heart.

I have great sympathy and affection for the builders in this book. They are driven by the same urge I feel, that many writers feel, that Carl Jung felt: to build the imaginary worlds we see in our heads, to get them out there so that others can see them. They are building a feeling, communicating an atmosphere, with blocks, as a poet does with words.

Minecraft allows people to express their pent up desire to change the world. It's a game where all you do is change the world. Whereas real life has become a game where all you do is not change the world.

Minecraft, in creative mode, gives us a space where changing the world is effortless, endless, unlimited. It is a dream of perfect malleability. A universe that loves us, that wants us to form it, that helps us to change it.

The last great real frontier, the American frontier, closed a hundred years ago. But Minecraft still shimmers into being ahead of us, endlessly, a dream of the eternal frontier.

And we turn up, not with an RV, a motorbike, a motorboat, and five aluminium chairs, but with a pickaxe, and the tiny, vital matchbox of our imagination.

And we build a cave, a hut, a city. We build the strange and wonderful houses we've seen in dreams.

And we find out who we really are.

— Julian Gough
Irish novelist and author of the 'End Poem'

9

# WELCOME TO BLOCK CITY

I remember as a child being on the set of a movie my father was in, which was being filmed in the Scottish Highlands. One day, I wandered off on my own while they were shooting. I walked through an ancient graveyard with crumbling, moss-covered gravestones, and as I passed between them I touched one. It was made of polystyrene. I was delighted by the artificiality of this re-creation of real life – something that appeared perfect from inches away, but was just a beautiful facade made out of nothing.

Video games affected me profoundly from an early age for much the same reason. The chance to explore any landscape you can think of, from rainbow-filled kingdoms to gritty post-apocalyptic wastelands, all conjured and re-created on screen, is endlessly entertaining and fascinating.

Sandbox games have become very popular in recent years, allowing players to create their own worlds and make their own game. And perhaps none is more popular than Minecraft®. The first moment I appeared in a land of grassy hills, walked towards a tree, punched it and was rewarded with a block of wood, I knew the possibilities were endless, and not because I could see any complexity: it was its simplicity that was so inspiring. Like digital LEGO®, Minecraft's blocks could be pieced together in infinite combinations and to any scale – the only limitations were imagination and patience.

For many, the proposition Minecraft puts forward of unlimited creative freedom on a grand scale is actually quite daunting, but for some it has been an outlet for their hidden talents and their dreams. It has brought together an incredibly diverse community from around the world and from every walk of life. I've always felt that gaming is a great leveller. It doesn't matter what you look like, how strong or old you are or what language you speak – none of that matters because when we play together we are all the same. You can build anything in Minecraft and you can build with anybody. The teams, partnerships and individuals I have encountered, fervently working to create their own virtual cities, are wildly different from one another, yet the level of organisation and the realising of these cohesive visions is quite breathtaking.

This book celebrates the very best Minecraft city creations ever built. Each chapter explores a different theme and interpretation of what a living community might look like, how people live and what they feel is important to city life.

Past civilisations have been painstakingly re-created, so from the Ancient Egyptians to the Roman Empire, the way we used to live has been reassembled block by block. Urban metropolises reflect the most recognisable re-creations of our everyday lives, with familiar buildings and architectural styles that echo our daily surroundings. At the other extreme, fantasy kingdoms and futuristic zones showcase extreme and imaginative ideas of how city life could be, in another place or another time. These are builds polarised between the most hopeful dreams of society and the threat of our slow demise.

The inspiration behind each city, how long they took to create and the details of how they were put together are documented in the pages of the book, along with tutorials that will help guide you when it comes to building creations of your own. So, whether you're a seasoned mega builder or are considering putting together the smallest hut, prepare to be inspired!

— Kirsten Kearney

11

# THE STORY OF MINECRAFT®

Minecraft is aptly named, as it's all about mining and crafting. You break and place blocks to create new things. The blocks are cubes that represent dirt, stone, wood, ores and water, which can be mined from the procedurally generated world you arrive in when you begin your game. This basic concept was released publicly as an unfinished game by Swedish programmer Markus 'Notch' Persson on May 17, 2009.

At first, this creative mode of play had no fixed purpose or guidance. Players simply broke blocks and placed them to create new structures, offering a sandbox gaming experience that encouraged emergent play – it was up to the players to decide what to do for themselves.

The one thing that is more fun than messing around in a game aimlessly is messing around in a game with your friends, so a multiplayer mode quickly followed. Notch then implemented a 'survival' mode, which gave the game a sense of danger and urgency. Building became a matter of necessity, as players needed to protect themselves from the dangers of zombies and skeletons in the night! Even at this early stage, more and more people were starting to notice the potential of this simple little game.

After a few mentions in the games press in September 2010, Minecraft's web server crashed under the weight of new players signing up. Notch made the game free to download at this point, to compensate players for the crash, but this only served to increase the number of new players signing up daily.

Then came the 'mega builders'. A 1:1 perfect replica of the Starship Enterprise created in Minecraft went viral, and as Twitter lit up with talk about the game and YouTube started to fill with new and ever more imaginative builds, its popularity increased exponentially. Regular updates meant that players felt they were a part of the development process of the game, leading them to suggest new and exciting ways to create structures.

With 16 million users registered before the game was even officially released, when it finally launched in November 2011 it was an instant hit, garnering a slew of awards. The game was a critical and commercial hit and went on to sell 54 million copies. The game boasts its own annual global convention, in its fourth year at the time of writing.

Minecraft has also been used as an educational and tech application by schools, universities and institutions around the world. The game is being used to create a full replica of the British Museum, including all of its exhibits.

# WHO ARE NOTCH AND MOJANG?

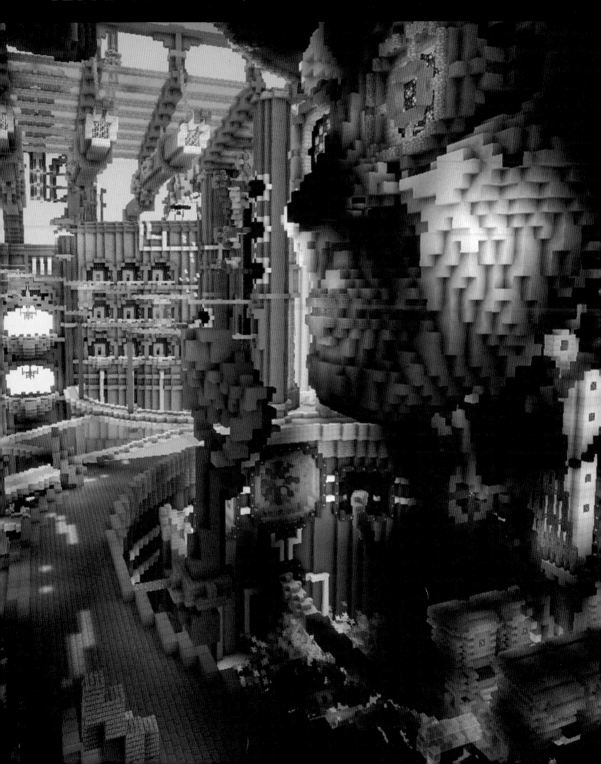

Born in June 1979, Markus 'Notch' Persson is a video game programmer and designer from Sweden. He began programming on a Commodore 128 when he was seven and had made his first game by the age of eight. When he began working in the game development industry he spent four years with King, the developer famed for the hit casual game, Candy Crush Saga.

Notch published a public beta of Minecraft® in 2009, which quickly gained attention and picked up a following. As the game continued to develop, more and more players signed up.

In September 2010, Notch founded the game development studio Mojang with his best friend, Jakob Porsér, with Carl Manneh coming in as CEO. The purpose of the company was to continue developing Minecraft, as well as branching out and creating new games. The company remained small, despite the increasing success of the yet-to-be launched Minecraft. Within a year, Mojang was running as a team of 12 and development had started on its second game, Scrolls. Before Minecraft officially launched, the company had generated $33 million (£21 million) and was fending off investment offers and lucrative financial deals in order to remain independent.

Mojang launched the full release of Minecraft in November 2011, at which point Notch stepped down from his role as lead developer on the game and Jens Bergensten took over.

The company is known for its humanitarian work, undertaking the Block by Block project in 2012. This project supported the United Nations Human Settlements Programme, with Minecraft players designing village and urban habitats in-game. The company also held a Humble Bundle Mojam event, raising $458,329.98 (£300,000) for four charities: Child's Play, Electronic Frontier Foundation, charity: water and the American Red Cross. During the event, Mojang's developers created a game in 60 hours, which was given to those who made a donation.

Notch has spoken out on several occasions about game piracy, antipiracy measures and the destructive force of big publishers on the games industry. However, he is not comfortable with the publicity and fame he has gained as the creator of one of the most popular games in the world.

When Mojang was sold in 2014, Notch, along with the other founding members of the team, Carl Manneh and Jakob Porsér, left the company. Notch made a statement saying that he does not see himself as a 'real' game developer and never intended or wanted to become a symbol of importance in the games industry. He plans to continue making games for fun, but if anything he makes ever gains any traction again he will likely abandon it immediately!

# WAYS TO PLAY MINECRAFT®

There are no set purposes, goals or challenges in Minecraft. Your world is procedurally generated from a seed when first created, at which point you can specify details by adjusting the biomes within it, such as desert, jungle and snowfield areas. The world will also be populated with animals, villagers and hostile creatures. The difficulty level can be altered, which includes a peaceful level that removes all hostile creatures.

There are three modes of play: survival, creative and adventure. In survival mode, the player has a health bar, which can be depleted by hostile creatures known as 'mobs' that mostly come out at night and attack the player. It's also possible to burn, suffocate or even starve if you don't find and eat food. When a player starts in survival mode the main priority is to create a shelter by nightfall. By acquiring resources through mining, you can craft tools and armour to protect against

mobs and increase the speed at which resources can be mined. Some players like to build large structures and cities in this mode, which is challenging, as resources have to be mined manually and the player has to manage his or her health.

Creative mode focuses on building by removing the health and hunger bars and giving full access to all of the in-game resources and items in infinite quantities, without having to mine or craft them. The player can also fly in this mode, which makes building a much easier process.

Adventure mode allows players to create custom maps specifically for others to play out a scripted adventure. The command block allows the creator to input server commands for the player to interact with.

# MINECRAFT LORE

Despite the simplicity of the Minecraft world and the lack of a driving purpose behind the player's actions, an extensive lore has built up around the game and its community. Naturally occurring phenomena of the game's coding helped inspire the imaginations of players.

A perfect example of this is the Far Lands. The maps were originally designed by Notch to be infinitely large, so they were generated as the player travelled through them. However, if a player teleported a certain distance from the centre of the map they would reach a point where the terrain starts to break up and the world ceases to function properly. Shrouded in darkness and attracting hostile mobs, the Far Lands were a dangerous place. The player's movement through the area shudders and stutters as massive amounts of sand and gravel fall, slowing the game to a crawl.

However, the Far Lands no longer exist in the current version of the game, having been patched out in an update some time

ago. Despite this, one player – Kurt J. Mac – continues to walk through the Far Lands using an older version of the game. He has been making his way to the edge of the world on foot, with a pickaxe, a sword and a compass, for four years – it could take him another 20 years to arrive at 'the edge'. You can follow his journey on his YouTube channel, Far Lands or Bust. So far he has raised $269,000 (£178,000) for the charity Child's Play in this quest through viewer donations.

The Overworld is not the only place to explore in the game. It is possible to create a portal from an obsidian frame that will transport you to the Nether, a hellish, cave-like world filled with lava and special Nether-only hostile mobs, items and blocks. Maps, clocks and compasses do not work in this dangerous dimension – try sleeping in a bed and it will explode!

Another portal you must find, repair and activate will take you to a dimension called the End. In this empty plane, with a planet-like island and starless sky, you must fight the Ender Dragon to receive the reward of a dragon egg and then escape. If you manage this you will see game credits as though you have 'finished' the game.

While the End makes a pretence at some kind of structure to gameplay in Minecraft®, it's the player's emergent behaviour that gives real structure to the game. One of the most popular player-created games is Spleef, a multiplayer arena game where the goal is to be the last player standing as each tries to destroy the blocks beneath their opponents, who fall into a pit below.

These are just a few of the many aspects of Minecraft's lore, but the most important and pervasive emergent element of the game is 'legend' – a myth that will not die. The character of Herobrine looms large in the minds of Minecraft players, but that is the only place where he looms large, because there is no such character. The story of Herobrine has spread through the community: an entity, a ghost or maybe even a demon, he is rumoured to be the dead brother of Notch, existing in purely digital form, stripping trees of their leaves and creating strange in-game structures such as sand pyramids. He is depicted as looking like the default character model 'Steve' but with white eyes. Notch and Mojang have released several statements denying the existence of Herobrine, although not all of them have been particularly helpful in killing off the myth.

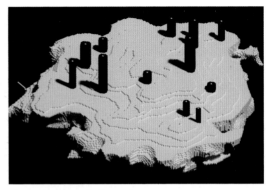
The End, home of the Ender Dragon

The Nether – a hellish, cave-like, lava-filled world

'There certainly are NO physical manifestations of Herobrine that will sneak out of your computer if you leave Minecraft running at night, looming over you as you sleep with his pale eyes inches away from your face, as he tries to shout at you to wake up. Sometimes you wake up with a jolt, and he's gone, and all that lingers is the memory and faint echo of his wordless screaming. Of course it was just a dream. There's no way a morally dubious ghost with a god complex could at any point decide to haunt the children who play my game "for their own good", as there is NO SUCH THING.'

– Markus 'Notch' Persson

# CHOOSING YOUR PLATFORM

The PC edition of Minecraft® is the natural platform of choice for mega builders who want to create the sort of epic cities and structures seen in these pages. It's possible to modify the game easily, adding new items and abilities to aid in the construction of complex builds. Some modifications or 'mods' allow you to copy and paste whole areas, so that buildings can be created once and then replicated and used over and over again.

The console version of Minecraft was developed by 4J Studios and is available for Xbox 360, Xbox One, PS3, PS Vita and PS4. While the map area is much smaller than that available on a PC, the most recent consoles (the Xbox One and PS4) allow a map size that is 36 times larger than the older generation versions. Packs are also available to download that offer new character skins, textures and themed worlds, although there is not the same ability to create and share community-made mods and packs, as there is on the PC version. However, if you use a console, the multiplayer game is considerably simpler to set up and take part in online, as a PC needs a server to be created. Minecraft can also be played in a four-player split-screen mode using a single console.

It would be easy to assume that the Pocket Edition of Minecraft (which is available for iOS, Android, Xperia and Amazon Fire devices) would run with inferior graphics to the PC and console versions. However, the mobile version actually boasts a more vibrant look and touch-screen controls. While it is not the ideal format for creating complex builds, this is still a challenge that many brave mega builders have undertaken, so it shouldn't be discounted.

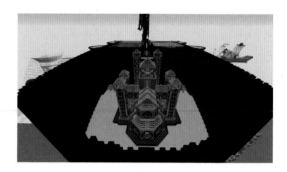

Obsidian Castle was built using the Xbox 360 console version of Minecraft. It is a medieval castle supported in the air by two walls, with two villages underneath that are split by a large water feature and garden. Builder Michael Newton's aim with Obsidian Castle was simply to make something big. It is an incredible achievement to have made this city on a console, as it can be tricky to build using console versions of Minecraft, which don't have the resource packs and render software available in other versions.

# TOOLS AND BLOCKS

There are hundreds of different types of blocks available in Minecraft®; some can be mined, such as ores and plants, while others are manufactured by crafting them. Items such as tools can also be crafted to speed up the mining process. All tools have a durability and will take damage the more they are used. Wood, stone, iron and diamond tools have increasingly better durability and speed of use.

However, in creative mode all blocks and items are available in your inventory in infinite quantities. These are used by builders in all kinds of interesting ways to create structures and re-create recognisable 'real' items.

Below is a selection of the tools and materials that are available to you.

## TOOLS

| Compass | Diamond sword | Flint & steel | Gold axe | Iron spade | Item frame |
| Sign | Stone pickaxe | Water bucket | Wooden hoe | Lava bucket | Music disc |

## MATERIALS

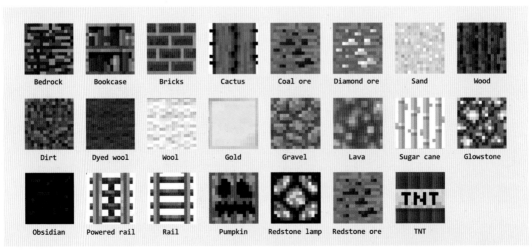

| Bedrock | Bookcase | Bricks | Cactus | Coal ore | Diamond ore | Sand | Wood |
| Dirt | Dyed wool | Wool | Gold | Gravel | Lava | Sugar cane | Glowstone |
| Obsidian | Powered rail | Rail | Pumpkin | Redstone lamp | Redstone ore | TNT | |

For builds set in the desert, sandstone is ideal.

Minecraft is all about creativity and imagination – this build uses various random materials, and the result is a colourful and interesting city.

Wood is the main material used in this steampunk-style world.

For sci-fi worlds, shiny or metallic-looking materials are best. This city has been built with quartz and glass.

# MODS

Mods add content to Minecraft®, giving the player more ways to interact with their world, changing the gameplay, mobs or available items, or improving ease of control.

While texture packs can give blocks a more detailed look, the most dramatic mods available to change the look of your builds are shaders. Shaders change the lighting, smoothness and particle effects, which can make a big difference to how your huge cityscapes look.

While mods such as shaders and texture packs can improve the look of your builds, editing tools such as World Edit and MCEdit can aid the building process itself.

WorldEdit is an in-game tool that allows you to select, replace or delete thousands of blocks at a time. It can also be used to modify the randomly generated terrains so that players can flatten a whole mountain. It is most useful to city builders as a way to copy and paste whole areas, so that one building can be replicated with the press of a button, rather than building from scratch each time.

MCEdit is an open-source world editor that was originally developed to allow players to preserve builds created in older versions of Minecraft and move them into newer versions of the game. Updates to the editor now allow players to use a 'brush' tool to paint blocks into shapes, scale objects, move spawn points and export objects.

Shaders can produce a variety of effects on the look of your game, without affecting the gameplay.

Biomes O' Plenty introduces a plethora of new environments to play in, as well as new blocks, trees and plants that you can populate your world with.

Mutant Creatures is a fun mod that allows mutated mobs to spawn in the game.

BuildCraft adds a whole new element of play, creating a chain of resources, crafting and construction that allows players to create vast factories and generators.

# FUNDAMENTALS

Minecraft® worlds feature distinct landscapes known as biomes, which fall into five different temperature categories. These are snowy, cold, dry, lush and neutral. Within these categories there are 61 distinct biome types offering a variety of looks and atmospheres.

When building in creative mode, selecting and landscaping a suitable biome for your style of build is important. Building can be made easier still by changing the weather and time of day so you are building on a bright, clear day, with the best view of what you're doing. No one likes building in the rain!

This idyllic pond, complete with water lilies, makes a great water feature.

## WATER

Water is an element that is often forgotten about when creating a large city, despite its fundamental importance to human existence. Building a city on a river is one way to bring water to your build, and most major cities in the real world are built close to a water source. However, even a small pond or fountain can help bring water to a landlocked area.

This ultramodern house features a living room built underwater.

# LIGHTING

If you are building during a sunny day it can be easy to get caught up in the shape and architecture of your buildings and forget that they need to be seen at night as well. Lighting is vital and should be incorporated into the structure of your building to illuminate it when night falls.

Lighting is also important in interiors. While windows will let in all the light you need during the day, at night your interiors will be plunged into darkness if you haven't planned ahead. Lighting in small spaces can be very harsh and detract from your beautifully designed rooms. Concealed lighting can provide a much more subtle and attractive look.

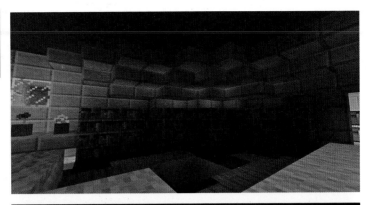

Top: A dark interior with insufficient lighting.

Second from top: Interior with glowstone lighting behind slabs.

Second from bottom: Interior with concealed lighting behind slabs.

Bottom: A well-illuminated building.

# BUILDING TIPS

Survival building is not for the fainthearted, with many players insisting that a real builder will mine their own resources while fending off hostile mobs. This can make building a fun – if lengthy – process, which becomes even more difficult if you are planning to build something as large as a city. For most players, working in creative mode and using mods such as WorldEdit is the most practical way of approaching an epic build.

While some of the tips given by the builders in this book contradict one another, there are some fundamental points that everyone agrees on. Researching your buildings and architectural style is one of the most important elements. If you are working on a modern building, then Google Maps Street View is an excellent resource for viewing buildings from around the world at different angles. For historic, fantasy and futurist builds, photographs of ruins, paintings and movies can prove invaluable in providing details you might never have considered for your particular type of building.

Most builders agree that a varied landscape is vital if you want to give your city an element of realism. Working with mountains and water around you can bring your city to life. Certain mods will also allow you to reform the land, literally 'moving mountains' (in a virtual sense at least).

There are certain decorations available in the game, such as carpets and bookshelves, but that does not mean you can only use those to bring details to your buildings. As you will see, a chair can be made from a simple stair block and signposts on either side for armrests. So, rather than think of game items as specific objects with a specific purpose, it can be better to think of them simply as shapes that can be placed together.

While re-creations of realistic cities and structures can be a great challenge and look hugely impressive, remember that Minecraft® is a game that takes little notice of the laws of physics. This means your themes don't have to follow the rules of the real world – you could easily create an underwater city, for example, or a giant hairdryer in the sky!

Here the builders Jakpok Cooperative have used ladders to act as vines to add realism to this Indiana Jones-inspired build.

# BUILDING TEAMS

While playing Minecraft® can be a solitary experience (and some of the biggest and best city builds are the vision and creation of highly talented individuals), the game has also brought about the emergence of an enormous community. Within this community, builders have come together to form teams that work to create complex cities. Some of these communities work on specific themes, such as the Broville team that has been working on a huge modern city for years, or WesterosCraft, which is dedicated to re-creating the continent of Westeros, as featured in the book series *A Song of Ice and Fire* and seen in the TV show *Game of Thrones*.

Larger teams will occasionally recruit new members and at other times close applications if the team has reached its maximum manageable capacity. Although some teams are worldwide organisations, which are quite loosely controlled, others are formed organically from groups of friends, some of which are small and local enough to meet in real life to discuss their plans, or are ruled with an iron pickaxe by one leader.

Although primarily formed to play together, many teams have developed into professional groups with huge YouTube followings who take commissions to create builds for businesses and even movie productions. Many teams even have business managers who negotiate advertising revenue and contract the use of build imagery in merchandise throughout the world.

Sanacraft is still a small and relatively unknown team, but their ambition is to establish themselves as one of the biggest creative building servers.

# BUILD THIS FIRST

There is no limit to what you can build in Minecraft®. If you are new to the game and just starting out, before you begin browsing the tutorials in this book, you might want to try out this simple project to help you get the hang of the building process. The steps involved in building this house are essentially the same for any kind of building, and once you become familiar with the process you can start adding additional details and creating more complex builds. The tutorials in this book aim to inspire you to find your own style.

**1**

## FLOORPLAN
Find an empty spot that is big enough for what you want to build. Mark out where the walls will be. You can use any type of block you want, depending on how you want the base of your house to look. This example uses stone.

**2**

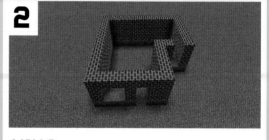

## WALLS
Stack the walls of your house, again using any type of block you want, such as wood planks, stone bricks, or bricks (as above). You can define the windows and doors at this stage or do it later if you prefer.

**3**

## FLOORING
Add flooring to your build so that you do not have grass inside your house. Here the floor is made with birch wood planks.

**4**

## WINDOWS
Create holes for your windows all around your build and add glass to them. Add a front door. The size of windows and doors can vary from one build to another.

**5**

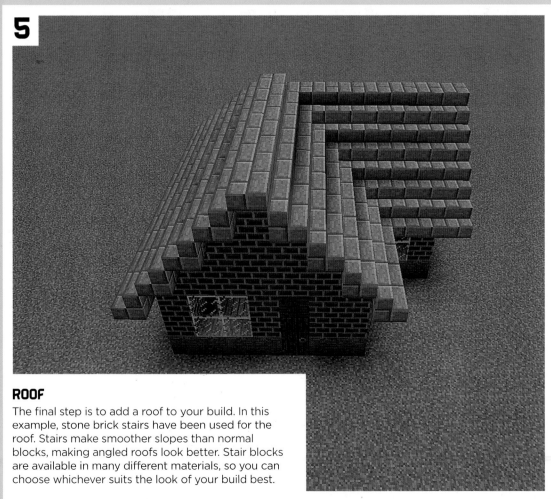

## ROOF

The final step is to add a roof to your build. In this example, stone brick stairs have been used for the roof. Stairs make smoother slopes than normal blocks, making angled roofs look better. Stair blocks are available in many different materials, so you can choose whichever suits the look of your build best.

# CITY TOUR GUIDE

Infinite varieties of cities have been created in the world of Minecraft®, and this book features some of the best builds falling under four different themes: Urban Metropolises, Fantasy Kingdoms, Futuristic Zones and Historic Realms. Each of these builds (shown here) includes a biography of the creator or team behind it, a description of the build and its inspiration, some statistics about how it was put together and a few of the mega builders' best tips. These city builders have also created tutorials on simple things related to or seen in their city that you can try building for yourself.

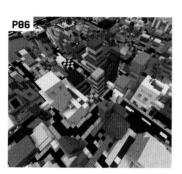

P86

P92

P102

P108

P114

P122

P126

P128

P132

P138

P148

P154

P156

P166

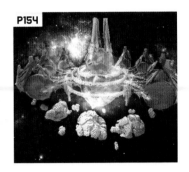
P174

P188

P186

P194

# CHAPTER 1

# URBAN METROPOLISES

# APPLE'S INFINITE LOOP HEADQUARTERS, CUPERTINO

**Mods:** WorldEdit
**Point of interest:** A command block on the map automatically sets the world time to 9.41 a.m., the time Apple puts on the clock in all advertising images for the iPhone.

Michael Steeber has been a fan of both Apple and Minecraft® for several years, so the idea to re-create Apple's headquarters in Minecraft was a natural one.

Michael was already fairly familiar with the general layout of the Apple campus, but still spent quite a bit of time researching to get all of the details right. Most of the build relied heavily on Google Maps Street View for photos of the campus's exterior, but it proved difficult to find out what certain interiors look like.

Some of the more notable features of the build are the company cafeteria, the extensive car parks (which have been replicated row by row and tree by tree), and BJ's Restaurant & Brewhouse, the next-door neighbour to the Apple campus and a favourite haunt of many employees. There is also a re-creation of the Apple Town Hall, Apple's on-site auditorium, where the first iPod was introduced to the world.

## THE BUILDER
Michael Steeber is 19 years old and from the United States. He currently writes and makes videos for the Apple blog *9to5Mac*, as well as creating videos for his own business, Chroma Videos. His interests are design, photography, videography, history and all things Apple.

In his spare time, aside from Minecraft, Michael enjoys working with Photoshop, studying history and listening to music. He likes creating Minecraft builds that are accurate re-creations of real-life structures. His specialities are 'old west' and abandoned buildings, and he is also a big fan of historical builds.

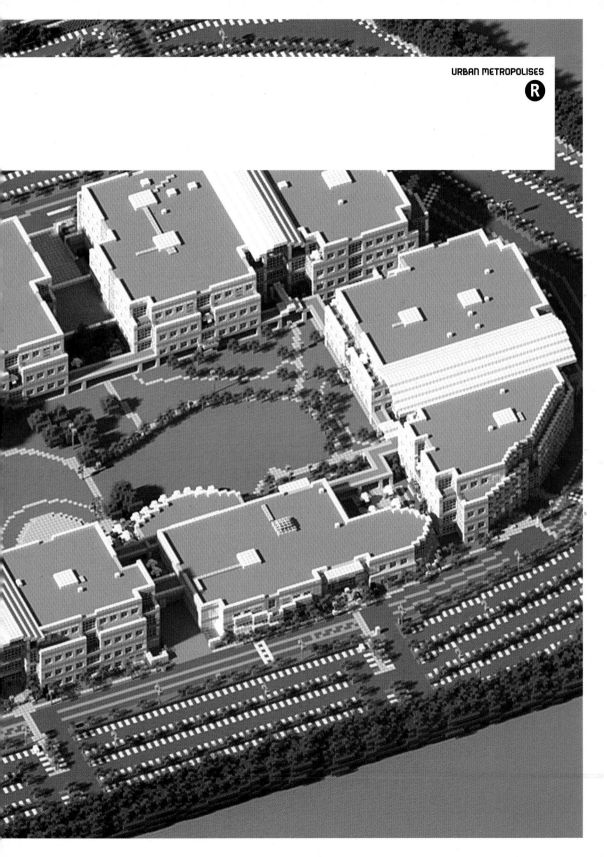

# OUTDOOR SEATING

When it comes to landscaping, the difference between a beginner and a pro is in the details. Something like a patio set can really make your landscape stand out, and it's easy to build. For this tutorial, quartz stairs are used for the patio umbrella, pistons form the table, and wooden stairs create the chairs. However, there are no set guidelines. It's up to you to decide which materials work best – this tutorial is just an introduction to landscape detailing.

**1**

## TABLE
Place five pistons in a cross shape on the ground to form your table. Put two fence posts on top of each other on the centre block of the table.

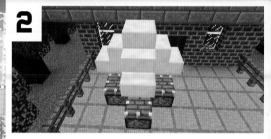

**2**

## UMBRELLA
Attach any type of stairs to the highest fence-post block. Make sure you have stairs on all four sides. Put a slab of the same material on top of the highest fence post.

**3**

## CHAIRS
Add chairs to your patio set. Wooden stairs work well, especially if you position one on each side of the table.

**4**

## DETAILS
For an extra touch of realism you can add arms to your chairs using signs. Place one sign on either side of each stair.

## MICHAEL'S TIPS

Start by establishing a unit of measurement for your build. For Apple's campus, the measurements were based on the estimate that one office window equals two blocks in width. Using this rule allowed everything on the building to remain in proportion.

Be creative with material usage. Around the perimeter of Apple's campus is a row of small trees, but even the smallest oak trees in Minecraft® are too large for the area. However, fence posts and leaves created realistic-looking saplings.

It's easy to get burned out very quickly on large projects. Don't force yourself to complete one piece of the build before you move on to the next or you risk losing interest in the whole project. Instead, start several areas of the map at once, and work on them all in shifts.

# AUDITORIUM

Auditoriums are typical landmarks in many cities, and Minecraft® cities are no exception. Giving your city an auditorium not only adds a nice detail, but also gives the area a certain authenticity and realism. Whether you have just a small space to build in or a large hall to fill, it's not too difficult to get started. There are numerous variations on this concept, so you can get very creative here. However, for this tutorial, we'll look at creating a medium-sized, classic auditorium.

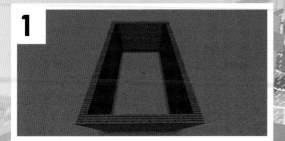

## BASIC STRUCTURE

You should begin this project with a space in mind. Start by building a basic four-wall structure.

## SEATING

Carve out the area for the auditorium's tiered seating, dropping one layer every two rows. Make sure to leave space in front for the stage. The stage should be the height of the third row of seating.

## WALLS AND FLOORING

Finish off the walls and flooring with whatever materials you'd like. Leave two blocks' space at each side of the room for stairs.

## BENCHES AND STEPS

Using your stairs of choice, add seating across each row. Using another stair type, inset steps into the aisles on each side of the auditorium and up to the stage.

## 5

## LIGHTING

Using redstone lamps, add in-floor lighting on each stair tier and at the top of the stage (levers underneath the lamps will provide power). Now is a good time to cut out a space for a doorway as well.

## 6

## CEILING

Make a ceiling for your auditorium, mirroring the tiered pattern of the floor (black wool works well for a dark ceiling). Add lighting in the ceiling as well, as described previously.

## 7

## STAGE DESIGN

Add a backdrop and overhead curtain for your stage. Regular wool works well as a backdrop if you're not sure what to use. A red curtain will give the auditorium the look of a cinema.

## 8

## FINISHING TOUCHES

Add some finishing touches, such as a podium or a table and chairs on the stage. Be sure to add an attractive entrance to your auditorium as well.

# CHICKEN COVE

Chicken Cove was originally planned as a refurbishment of an older project called Cove House, which was built in the 1.2 Beta release of Minecraft® and grew to become a luxury estate.

Inspired by the work of Ludwig Mies van der Rohe and a variety of other modernist architecture, the most important feature of the design is the construction of space using pillars and beams. This freely manageable space (known as 'universal space') enables the building to be expanded and furnished in an intuitive way.

Another important element of Chicken Cove is that it was designed to adapt to the randomly generated landscape created by Minecraft, rather than being built onto a landscape that had been completely flattened.

### THE BUILDERS
Yuki Lin is a 21-year-old university student studying architecture at the University of Sydney, Australia. Chicken Cove was created in collaboration with his friend, Reijo Wong.

With experience of living in Japan, Taiwan, Hong Kong, Vietnam, the United Kingdom and Australia, Yuki is inspired by human modification of the natural environment and was drawn to study architecture. As a world traveller, Yuki visualises structures that are not bound by cultural conventions.

Yuki's Minecraft builds lie somewhere between modernist and post-modernist in style, as they are designed to be functional, while also incorporating superfluous features and structures.

**Server:** pastel.mcserver.ws
**Shaders:** Sonic Ether's
Unbelievable Shaders

**Time to build:** Two weeks
**Blocks used:** Countless virtual chickens
were harmed in the making of this house.

# LIGHTING INTERIORS

This is one of the most effective ways to improve your build. An early champion of the technique was TrynePlague1.0, a player who used the Minecraft® 1.8 pre-release to light large contemporary housing without showing the harsh textures of glowstones.

Various types of indirect lighting have been discovered since – for example, it is possible to create indirect lighting by covering a light source with snow (although the snow melts unless you use specific plugins to prevent that from happening).

## GLASS TUNNELS

Identify an area to light, making sure you have a wall that is at least three blocks deep. Make a glass tunnel inside the wall to allow concealed light to come out. The difference between direct lighting and indirect lighting using glass is shown here.

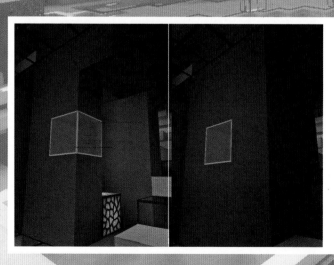

## EMBED LIGHTS IN WALLS

Lights can be embedded within walls.

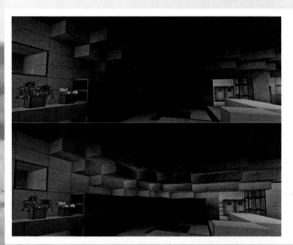

## MOOD EFFECTS

Any type of half slab lets some light through, but this is not enough to light a room adequately. Instead, it should be used with a combination of classic indirect lighting to add a mood effect to your build. Shown here is the effect before and after using slab indirect lighting. Note that you must use half slab blocks – full slab blocks will not allow any light through.

## HALF SLABS

Make sure there is always a gap of half a slab between half slabs and the light source. This technique is effective for lighting curved surfaces. This cut section of the ceiling shows one way to lay out slab indirect lighting.

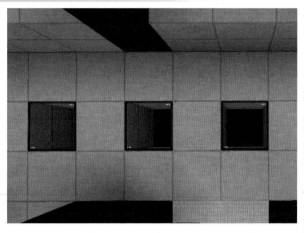

## LIGHTING FLOORS

An end portal can make a good substitute for a glowstone when it comes to lighting floors. It has a very interesting texture that will change depending on the angle it's seen from.

## END PORTAL LIGHTING

To create end portal floor lighting, spawn end portal blocks by placing them down and putting ender eyes into end portal frames, both obtainable in creative mode, and then remove the end portal frames after the portal has spawned. Here, the end portal frame has been removed and the end portal block is still there. You need to remove excess end portal blocks and cover with glass and other blocks to use as a light source.

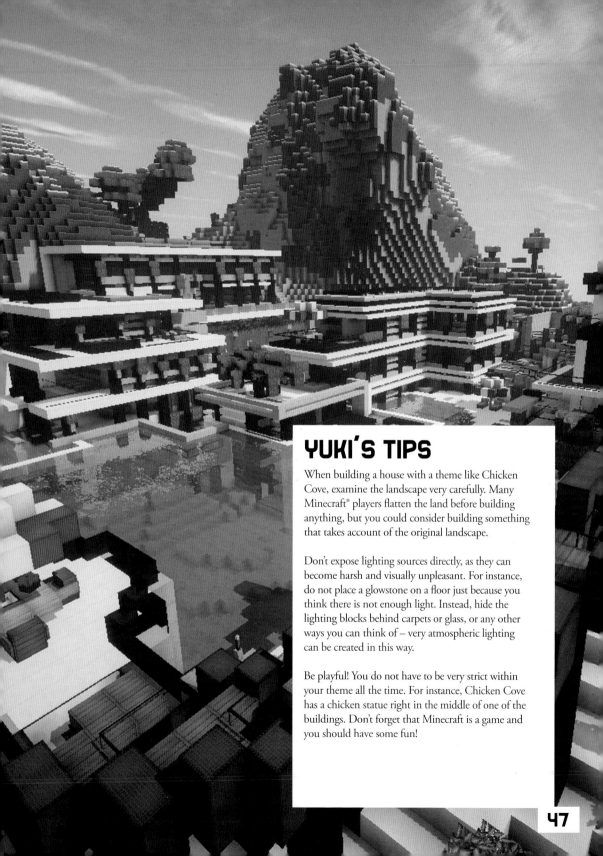

## YUKI'S TIPS

When building a house with a theme like Chicken
Cove, examine the landscape very carefully. Many
Minecraft® players flatten the land before building
anything, but you could consider building something
that takes account of the original landscape.

Don't expose lighting sources directly, as they can
become harsh and visually unpleasant. For instance,
do not place a glowstone on a floor just because you
think there is not enough light. Instead, hide the
lighting blocks behind carpets or glass, or any other
ways you can think of – very atmospheric lighting
can be created in this way.

Be playful! You do not have to be very strict within
your theme all the time. For instance, Chicken Cove
has a chicken statue right in the middle of one of the
buildings. Don't forget that Minecraft is a game and
you should have some fun!

# EMPIREPOLIS

**Server:** Vanilla Minecraft (private)
**Point of interest:** Contains more than a hundred buildings and towers, including famous US landmarks such as the United States Capitol Building and the Pentagon.

The aim of Empirepolis is to accurately create replicas of buildings and whole city blocks from major US cities, and it currently consists of areas inspired by Chicago, Atlanta, New Orleans, Los Angeles, Miami, New York and Washington, DC.

Empirepolis is a unique project that offers Minecraft® players the opportunity to wake up in New Orleans, venture a few blocks away to the wide boulevards of Los Angeles, and take a walk down Hollywood Boulevard to end up in Washington, DC. While it looks like one big city, the contrasting architecture of the major US cities subtly flows from one style to another.

While Google Maps and Google Earth were used to research the exteriors, most of the interiors of Empirepolis were created from the builders' imaginations. Exceptions are the most famous interiors – such as Grand Central Station in New York – which are faithfully re-created.

The team has used its build as a conduit to learning about the history and geography of the cities it is re-creating. As a result, the builders are certain they would never get lost in the real New York, even though they've never been there!

### THE BUILDERS

František Hanzlík is 22 and works for a small steel company in the Czech Republic. His building partner is 15-year-old student Blair Miles from Louisiana in the United States. While coming from completely different backgrounds, their shared passion for creating realistic builds in Minecraft has brought them together online.

František started work on this project in early 2012 and was soon discovered by Blair, who wanted to help out when he discovered that František was working alone. As Blair was only 13 years old at the time, František's expectations were low – until he saw Blair's perfect replica of New Orleans's One Shell Square skyscraper. They now work in partnership, with František working primarily on exteriors and Blair creating the buildings' interiors.

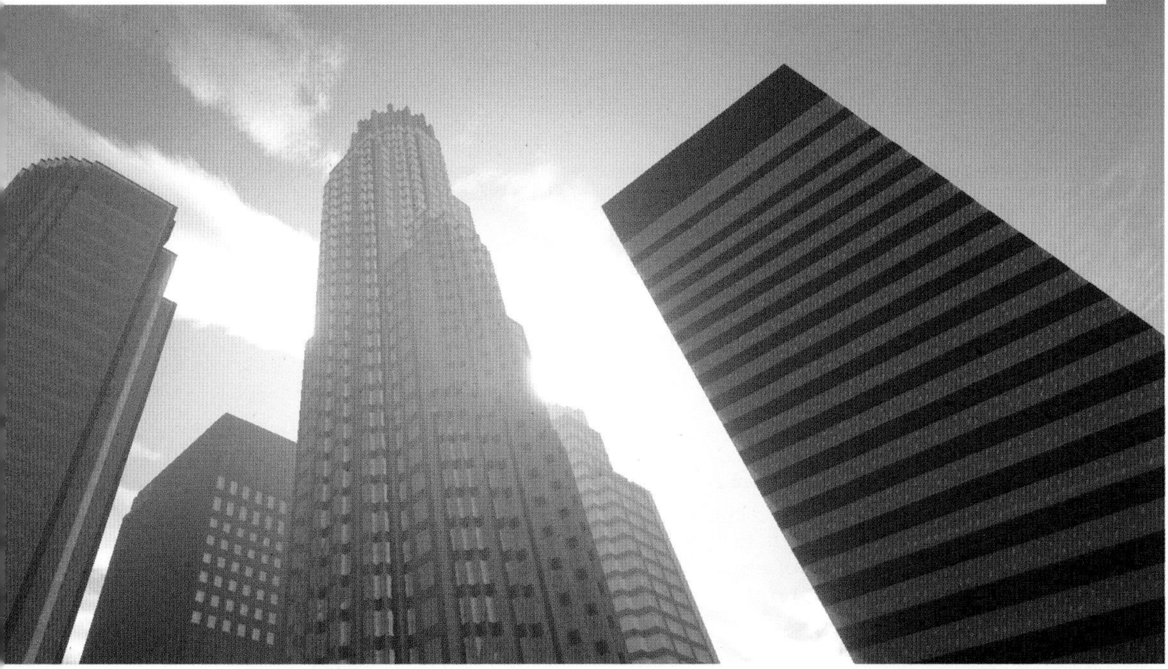

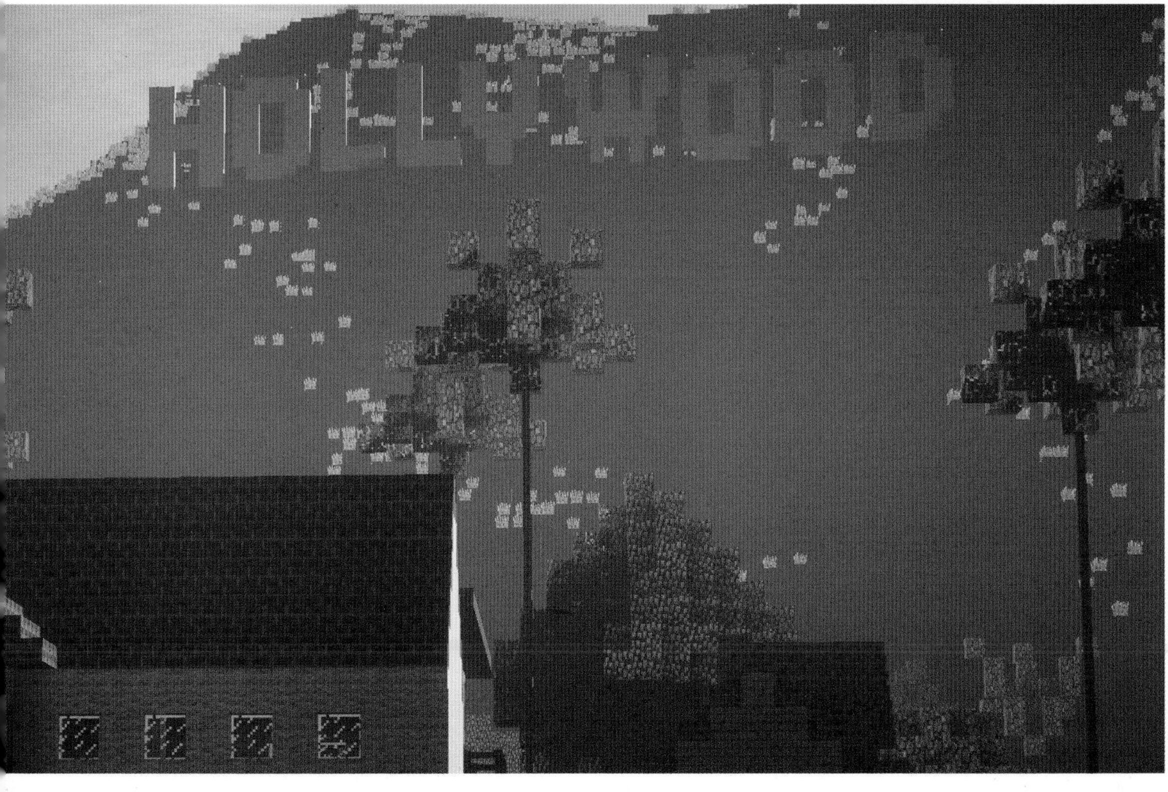

# FIRE ESCAPE

Fire escapes are a type of emergency exit, commonly seen on the outside of apartment buildings in big cities in the United States. They are quite easy to make in Minecraft® and can give a subtle touch of realism to a build.

## 1

### BASE
Make the base of the fire escape long enough so that a player could go downstairs and not hit the floor. For this tutorial we are using stone slab blocks, four blocks long.

## 2

### HANDRAIL
Create the handrail next. Don't place it exactly on the stone slab blocks, as it will be in the way when the player tries to walk along the blocks.

## 3

### STAIRS
The stairs require a little patience because when you place the stair block, it is not always facing the direction you need it to.

## 4

### LOWER BASE
Make an identical base to the one you created in step 1, and add a handrail as detailed in step 2.

**5**

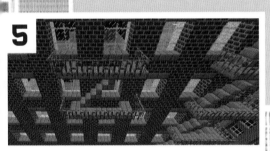

## ADDITIONAL LEVELS

Create additional levels, depending on how many floors your building has.

# FRANTIŠEK'S TIPS

If you want to create a building in Minecraft® that looks like the real thing, use several sources for inspiration, so you can study the architecture from all angles. You will also need to carefully consider the materials you're going to use – Minecraft is unlikely to have blocks that are an exact match to the colour you need, so you will often have to make do with the closest match possible.

You can't build an entire city block by block – it would take a lifetime! MCEdit is a great tool that will allow you to build much faster. Using a tool like this you can create the ground floor of a skyscraper (block by block), then copy it using MCEdit to create a multifloor stack.

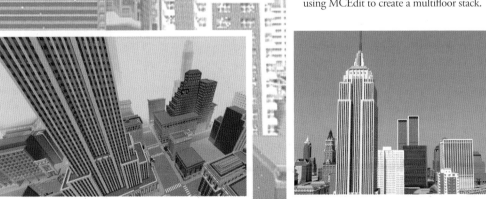

# BROWNSTONE HOUSE

In the real world, terraced row houses are built with brownstone, limestone and brick. They are typical for East Coast cities in the United States and are such a highly recognisable part of the New York landscape that no re-creation of a New York neighbourhood would be complete without them.

## 1

### FLOORPLAN
Plan the width of your building based on how wide you want the windows to be. Build the first line of walls.

## 2

### BASEMENT
The basement of a row house is often a different colour from the rest of the building. This example utilises green clay blocks. Build your basement six blocks high.

## 3

### COLUMN DETAIL
For a more realistic look, create columns behind the front wall. The windows will be placed between them. If they were placed in the front wall, the structure would look less detailed.

## 4

### FINISHING THE BASEMENT
Fill the empty spaces with windows and a front door. Build one line of green clay blocks above the basement. On the front side of the line, place stone brick stair blocks.

## 5 FIRST FLOOR

The first floor should be built from brick blocks, five blocks high.

## 6 SHAPING WINDOWS

Use brick stair blocks to complete the shape of the windows.

## 7 WINDOW PANES

Having used stair blocks, the windows cannot use glass pane blocks, as the window would seem to have holes. Instead, make a second line of wall behind the front one using grey clay blocks for more detail. Then, fill with glass blocks.

## 8 WINDOW LEDGES

Put stone slab blocks into each window on the front side of the building to create window ledges.

## 9

### MULTIPLE FLOORS

Row houses are usually three or four floors high. This particular building has the first floor one block higher than the others.

## 10

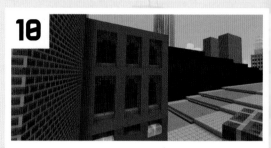

### FLOOR HEIGHTS

Subsequent floors should be one block shorter than the first.

## 11

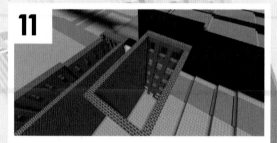

### JOINING WALLS

Joining walls don't need to be detailed.

## 12

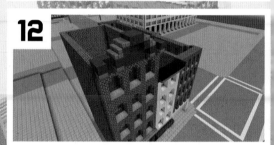

### TOP LEDGE

All row houses have a pediment, which is perhaps their most beautiful feature. This one has an arched pediment.

## 13

### FIRE ESCAPES

Now, add fire escapes, as detailed on pages 50–51.

## 14

### FRONT FACE

The completed facade should look similar to this.

## 15

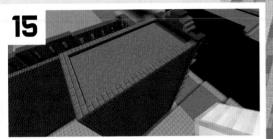

### ROOF

Use stone blocks for the roof to give an impression of concrete.

## 16

### DETAILS

To add detail, create an air conditioner using iron blocks in a four block square, with rails on them.

## 17

### STAIRWELLS

Create stairwells inside the building that go to apartments in the upper floors from the space in the basement.

## 18

### STAIRWELL CLOSE-UP

This is how the stairwell should look.

## 19

### FINISHED ROW HOUSE

The final brownstone building, complete with fire escapes.

# GREENFIELD CITY

**Server:** Greenfield Build Server
**Time to build:** Three years so far
**Blocks used:** 1.4 million blocks square

In 2011, Oskar created the first few buildings in Greenfield City, which can still be seen in the build today. Although he started work alone, he quickly recruited a number of friends and opened the server to applicants who wanted to help out; there are now 300 players on the list. Oskar wanted players to feel that they are walking around a real city, so every detail is designed carefully, right down to the smallest alleyway. The city even has a fictional history, so each area has its own style. Certain parts of the city appear abandoned, for example, while others are well developed and upmarket, but all have a story behind their condition.

## THE BUILDER

Oskar is a 20-year-old aspiring audio engineer from Manchester, England. He has a lifelong love of creating buildings and cities, which started with LEGO® bricks in his childhood, before he moved on to the early SimCity games and then Minecraft®. Oskar's first creation in the game was a city that he built with his brother. He built several more before starting the vast Greenfield City project.

# OSKAR'S TIPS

In a build like this, realism comes before anything. Sometimes you have to build a simple, grey, box-like building just because it's realistic – many buildings are little more than grey boxes.

Tiny details can affect your build – something small, such as a wall being out of line, can have a dramatic effect. You also need to consider how well your city balances as a whole. Does that skyscraper work next to that housing area? Is that building too wide or too thin? These things matter.

# OFFICE BLOCK

If you want a completely realistic building that is perfectly symmetrical, this is a good building technique. The Greenfield City builders are not looking to create architectural masterpieces – in real life not every building is a masterpiece, especially those built in the 1960s and '70s!

Build in 3x3, 4x4 or 5x5 cubes, so that everything will align perfectly using this 'cube method'. Floors will be five blocks tall for the lobby, and three blocks tall for the others. Using WorldEdit is very useful for buildings like this.

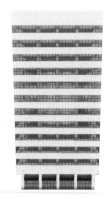

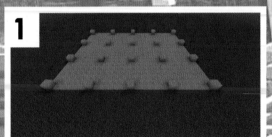

## 1

### FOUNDATION
Start with 12 cubes of 5x5 blocks. Measure them out on the ground and check that they all line up. Place blocks at the corners of the cubes.

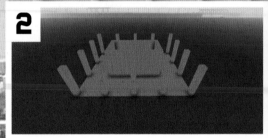

## 2

### LOBBY
Raise the blocks up to cover the lobby. Encase the central two squares in walls; you will use those as the building's core, which will house the lift and stairwell.

## 3

### FLOORING
Add flooring and repeat the previous steps to create a second floor.

## 4

### BUILDING FRAME
Continue adding floors until your building reaches the desired height. This will complete the building's frame, which you will work from.

## 5

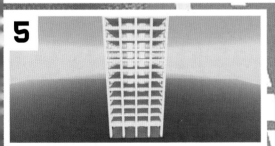

### OUTSIDE WALLS

Here is when WorldEdit is especially handy. Choose your materials: quartz has been used for this building.

## 6

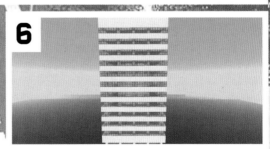

### FINISHING TOUCHES

Add the exterior and decorations. Here cyan glass is used with the quartz, as the colours complement each other well. Complete the interior and decoration inside too.

# APARTMENT BLOCK

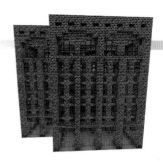

This is an early-20th-century apartment building that forms part of a city block building. As with the office block on pages 58–59, it is built using the cube method, although the side walls can be left blank to allow buildings to be attached to each other.

## 1

### FOUNDATION
Lay out your building shape. Measure it out in cubes of 3x3 blocks to allow detail and shaping.

## 2

### FRAME
Use a simple frame to build the front of the building to your chosen height.

## 3

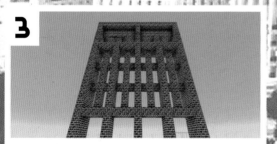

### CREATE DEPTH
To create depth and allow space for details, expand the building face one block out.

## 4

### DETAIL
Add basic details using slabs and stairs. This works particularly well on older-style buildings.

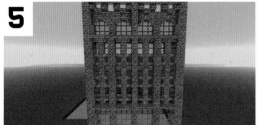

## 5

### WINDOWS

Add more detail and windows. This building uses white stained windows for a Victorian look.

## 6

### REMAINING WALLS

Transpose the exterior to the rest of the sides. The style can be alternated on different parts, but make sure it makes sense with the original design.

## 7

### INTERIORS

Use the 3x3 cubes to design an interior and build the walls, floors and stairs.

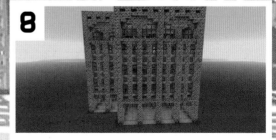

## 8

### FINISHED BUILDING

When your main building structure is complete, it should be perfectly symmetrical.

# HUNTINGTON CITY

**Server:** Esterlon Community Server
**Shaders:** Chunky (Rendering Program)
**Time to build:** Six months

Huntington is an imaginary city situated on an imaginary island country off the east coast of Canada and the United States. It's mainly a suburban city with aspects of American urbanisation, but with a European feel in the city centre, as it features a historic downtown core, while still boasting a vibrant central business district with modern buildings and skyscrapers.

Huntington Metropolitan Area is situated on a bay on the island's west coast with many rivers flowing into it. Because of the region's position in the world, the mountains around it are very cold during most of the year and the city itself has weather ranging from temperate to cold and rainy.

The planning and construction of the region was carried out by different members of the Esterlon build team, each specialising in distinct areas such as commercial, residential, industrial districts, transportation networks, rural areas and so on. Thanks to the expertise of all the members, Esterlon has been able to achieve great realism in the region, with more to come as the city continues to develop.

### THE BUILDERS

Yazur Strovoz (Joey Girard) is a professional Minecraft® builder. He is 16 years old and lives in Quebec, Canada. Yazur is one of the rare realistic city builders popular on Reddit, DeviantART and Planet Minecraft for his many builds.

Yazur and MancoMtz (Raul Martinez) are the proud owners of the Esterlon Community Server and building team, which has consisted of 400 members over its lifespan between the ages of 14 and 30 years old, from Canada, America, Mexico, Australia and Germany. The team began with the project Lapiz Point (see pages 64–65), with builders from around the world joining the server, which was called Alphacraft at the time. As the community grew, along with the team's skills, they decided to create a new city, Huntington. Around that time the team and server changed their name to Esterlon and formed the current makeup of the community. Esterlon's goal is to create the most realistic city in Minecraft.

# LAPIZ POINT CITY

**Server:** Esterlon Community Server
**Shaders:** Chunky (Rendering Program)
/ SEUS shaders
**Time to build:** One and a half years

Lapiz Point City was designed to be a modern, realistic city, based on Montreal and New York City. The downtown area was moved to a bigger map three months after its creation, when the builders realised the city was going to become bigger than first intended. The city grew slowly as the downtown and suburban areas evolved, with new builders joining the project having seen its development through images posted on the DeviantART and Planet Minecraft websites. As the team grew, the quality of Lapiz Point got better and better.

The city features an industrial area, a port, an airport, a number of bridges, two stadiums, a shopping mall and more than 200 homes and 300 buildings. A download link for the Lapiz Point Project and the texture pack is available online. There have been 2,000 downloads of the city and 50,000 of the texture pack.

### THE BUILDERS

Lapiz Point City was built by the Esterlon Community Team, originally called the Alphacraft Team, which was founded by Yazur Strovoz (Joey Girard) and MancoMtz (Raul Martinez). The team have since moved on to a new project – Huntington City (see pages 62–63).

The team consists of multiple builders who all specialise in different areas of building. One of MancoMtz specialities is infrastructure; he created the roads around Lapiz Point, designing highways and interchanges. Yazur is particularly well known for his vehicles, including cars, planes, helicopters and boats.

# MOTOR CAR

Cars are a good build to test out your skills with. The great thing about building cars in Minecraft® is you can get creative with the materials you use. In this project quartz is used to make the bodywork – it's the closest you'll get to the metallic shine real cars have – as well as black and grey windows on the sides to give the doors definition.

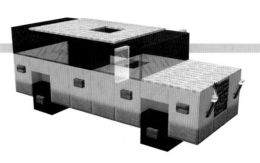

## 1
## WHEELS
Place your wheels. Make sure you have four blocks between the front wheels and the back wheels. Add stone buttons to each wheel for the hubcaps.

## 2
## CHASSIS
Use stone slabs for the frame of the car. You can use wood slabs or other materials, depending on what colour you want your car to be.

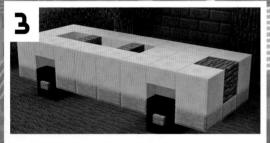

## 3
## BODYWORK AND INTERIOR
For the bodywork, you can again use any material, depending on what colour you want the car to be. Quartz is good for a metallic coat. Place stairs above the wheels and place an iron block or acacia wood log at the front for the grille.

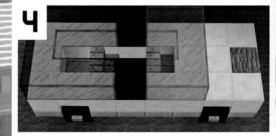

## 4
## WINDOWS
For the windows, use black stained glass at the back of the car and light stained glass at the front.

## 5

### BACK LIGHTS AND BOOT
For the back lights of your car use torches. Add a spare tyre for detail.

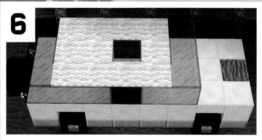

## 6

### ROOF
Fill the inside of your car with string to support the roof. Now place down carpet that matches your car colour and leave a hole for a sunroof.

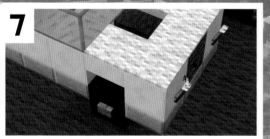

## 7

### ENGINE AND BONNET
You can use an anvil for the engine of the car for realism. Place wool on the bonnet to cover the engine.

## 8

### FINISHING TOUCHES
For additional detail, add buttons to your car as door handles and sidelights. You can also add mirrors as wing mirrors.

# HOUSE

Whether you want to build towers as tall as the sky, or grand buildings with wing after wing, a two-storey house is a good project to get to grips with the basics of building construction. Always start by laying your foundations. This helps you plan the structure of your building and the layout of the interiors.

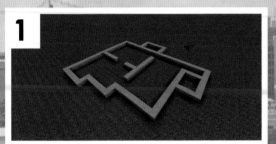

### 1

### FLOORPLAN
To build a house, you need a floorplan. Start by making the inside walls, so you can plot the rooms of the house. Factor in a kitchen, a living room and a dining room on the first floor.

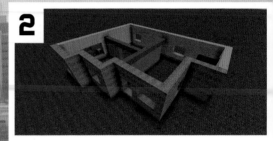

### 2

### WALLS
With your floorplan in place you can start stacking the walls. Use different materials for the inside and outside walls, such as coloured wood and clay. Leave holes for windows and doors.

### 3

### FLOORING
Lay down wooden planks for your flooring and stairways. Use quartz or something resembling tiles for the kitchen and bathrooms.

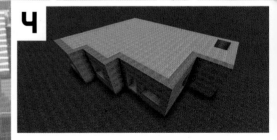

### 4

### SECOND STOREY
With your staircase in place you can lay down the floor for your second storey. Make sure you leave space at the top of the staircase.

## 5

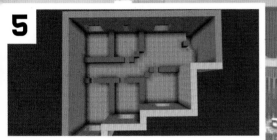

### SECOND-STOREY FLOORPLAN

Again, plot out your floorplan. Stack your walls, and when complete, lay down a ceiling using wood or wool. You can use glowstone or redstone lamps as ceiling lights.

## 6

### WINDOWS

With the main structure of the house complete you can begin work on smaller details, such as the windows. Put fences in the middle and upside-down quartz stairs above them.

## 7

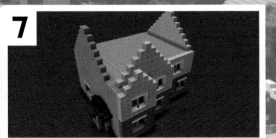

### ROOFING

Make the roof walls first, using the same materials as you did for the walls of the house. Add quartz slabs to the flat areas to act as gutters. You can use other slabs too.

## 8

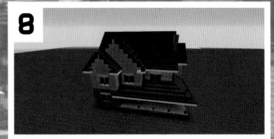

### PORCH AND ROOFING

Using wood for the deck, now build a porch. Add beams to support the roof and use quartz for the gutter. Use stairs to complete the roofing of the house and the porch.

### 9

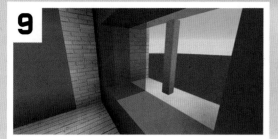

## INNER WINDOWS

From inside, add a layer of blocks against the wall to support your windows. Add glass.

### 10

## CHIMNEY

Using bricks, you can add a chimney to the side of your house. Use pots for the vents.

### 11

## PATIO AND VERANDA

Finish off the groundwork with a patio for the back garden and an adjoining veranda. You can add details to your patio like tables and chairs.

### 12

## FRONT DOOR

Lastly, build a front door out of any material you like. Your house is now ready and you can invite your friends around!

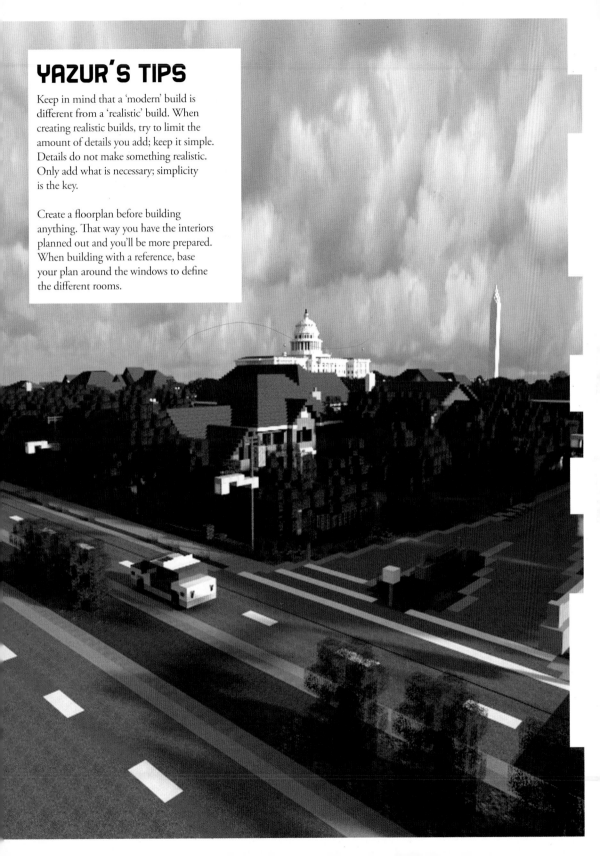

# YAZUR'S TIPS

Keep in mind that a 'modern' build is different from a 'realistic' build. When creating realistic builds, try to limit the amount of details you add; keep it simple. Details do not make something realistic. Only add what is necessary; simplicity is the key.

Create a floorplan before building anything. That way you have the interiors planned out and you'll be more prepared. When building with a reference, base your plan around the windows to define the different rooms.

# MATTUPOLIS

**Server**: Bukkit (local)
**Shaders**: Sonic Ether's Unbelievable Shaders
**Mods**: WorldEdit, VoxelSniper, MCEdit
**Time to build**: Three years
**Blocks used**: Wool, stained clay, slabs,
wood, stone, stone bricks, sandstone, end
stone, glass, ice, glowstone, and obsidian

The aim of Mattupolis was to develop a realistic urban environment in Minecraft®. Tired of playing the game's survival mode, Matias began working on a city, which has grown at a steady rate over the last three years.

Matias has drawn inspiration from a variety of urban concepts and styles. Originally, Mattupolis was a re-creation of New York, with Broadway and Central Park in place. However, once the downtown area had been built, Matias shifted his interests towards European architecture and then gradually moved back to North American building styles. Currently, it is Vancouver that inspires most of the project's additions.

While this is an incredibly time-consuming project (and still far from Matias's ultimate goal of a truly sprawling metropolis), he believes his plan is achievable. He sees Mattupolis as being past the point of no return and plans to continue until the work is done! The project has increased Matias's knowledge of architecture, which he feels will help him in his future studies.

### THE BUILDER
Matias Buks is 17 years old and attends high school in the sleepy rural town in western Finland where he lives. Minecraft is his most time-consuming hobby, but he is also a keen photographer and gamer.

When it comes to art, Matias likes to test his creative abilities and try new things with an open mind. Eventually, Matias plans to become an architect and has an ambition to make Finnish cities less drab. He also wants to travel the world, with a particular interest in visiting Canada and Sweden.

# ROUNDABOUT

Roundabouts are a common sight in today's urban areas, and they are growing in number across the United States faster than ever before. Some think it's a great junction design that improves road safety, while others feel they are confusing and rather dangerous. One thing is certain, though – they are round, and anything that breaks the Minecraft® norm of blockiness is good!

Any Minecraft metropolis can benefit from a few roundabouts. They really contribute to the realism of a cityscape, as do curved roads. They work best in the spacious outskirts of the city, surrounded by acres of grass and the car parks of shopping centres. However, before construction, consider the scale – a tiny roundabout in the middle of a busy motorway isn't something you'd expect to see.

## 1
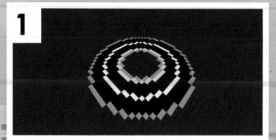

### CENTRAL ISLAND
Create a series of concentric circles to form the central island, the lane divider marking and the outer edge of your roundabout. If you're struggling, research 'Voxel Circles' online.

## 2
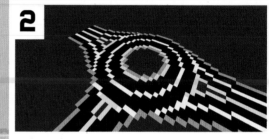

### CURVED ROADS
If you're inexperienced at creating curved roads, you may prefer to connect the roads directly, with no curves at all. However, your traffic circle will look a little less realistic.

## 3
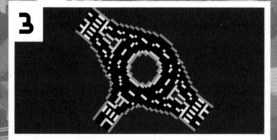

### ROAD MARKINGS
Add the necessary road markings, including crossings.

## 4

### FINISHING TOUCHES
For added realism, you might want to add plants, street lighting and perhaps some paving, complete with hedges.

# MATIAS'S TIPS

Before beginning work on a new district or entire city, plan ahead! Draw a rough illustration of your plan using something like Dynmap. Even if the end result doesn't match your original plan, it may be more successful than a fully improvised build.

Google Earth and Street View are useful when re-creating real-life cities in Minecraft® and can help pin down the finer details of a building. They are particularly useful for measuring when you are building to scale.

If you're not completely satisfied with a structure, don't destroy it! Save it as a schematic. It might come in handy at a later time.

# COMMIEBLOCK

One thing an urban metropolis needs is housing for the masses! Commieblocks are relatively easy to build, as the floorplan is usually simple and there's generally little variety between the floors.

The best thing about making these in Minecraft® is that you can experiment with different blocks and add interesting details to an otherwise nondescript structure – sometimes the end result can look quite pretty!

Before starting, pick a few blocks to use. Wool, bricks and sandstone are common options. Pay attention to scale as well. A little planning always makes things easier.

## 1

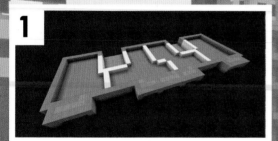

### FLOORPLAN
Start by laying out the base of the building. Don't forget to leave space for stairwells. There will be two of them in this building.

## 2

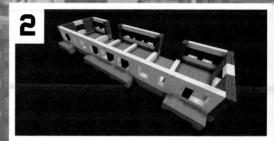

### EXTERIOR WALLS
Construct the outer walls using the blocks you chose earlier. Leave openings for windows and for doors leading to the balconies.

## 3

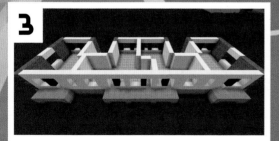

### FLOORING
Build walls dividing the apartments and lay down flooring. Birch planks are used here, but any other type of wood or light grey wool will work well.

## 4

### STAIRWELLS
Fill in the spaces left for stairwells with stair blocks all the way up to the second floor. Add doors leading to each apartment at this point.

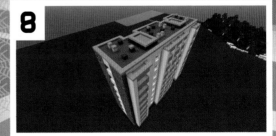

## 5

## BALCONIES

Add doors leading to each balcony, and once your first floor is finished, fill in the flooring for the second floor.

## 6

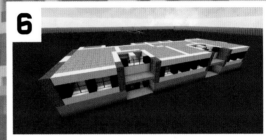

## GLASS PANES

Use normal glass for balconies and stairwells, but glass panes for the rest of the facade.

## 7

## MULTIPLE STOREYS

Copy and paste the floor you have built as many times as necessary to take the building to its finished height. This block has eight floors. You can use WorldEdit or a similar tool for this step.

## 8

## ROOFING

Finish off the building by adding a roof. This one uses grey stained clay. For extra realism, add air vents and other blocky items to the rooftop.

# PROJECT ZEARTH

**Mods:** NPC by Noppes
**Texture pack:** Mixcraft HD by Koolwitak
**Renders:** http://golonkaswe.tumblr.com/
**Time to build:** Five years
**Number of buildings in the map:** 300
**Torches used:** 152,293

Builder Yashar's original plan was to make a pyramid in Minecraft®, but seeing another city map in the game, called Broville, inspired him to build a far more complex urban metropolis. Consequently, Yashar's original pyramid turned into a temple, which then turned into several temples. Roads were added between them, a few buildings cropped up by the sides of them and a downtown area was developed. Far from these areas, whole new cities were built and then connected together with railways and roads. Now, every street has its own personality and there are hidden treasures, posters, secret paths, temples and villages dotted around as well.

Zearth is an endless project, with no ultimate plan. Yashar continues to add every new idea he has and improve on every part of the city, constantly adjusting things to accommodate new buildings and structures.

Five years into building, Zearth now contains a mix of old and new buildings. Occasional renovations are needed and new styles emerge, with more modern buildings cropping up all over the city.

### THE BUILDER
Yashar Irandoust (aka Xoyjaz) is a 19-year-old chemistry student from Norway. Despite not liking the look of it very much, Yashar started playing Minecraft on the recommendation of a friend in 2009. Although he was playing every day, building was a very slow process because Yashar's computer wasn't quite up to the required specifications. Having not backed up his save of the map he was working on when the game was first updated, Yashar lost all his work and vowed to quit playing.

However, before he quit, Yashar wanted to create a pyramid that he had a very clear design for in his mind. Inspired by 'Oldshoes', the creator of the Broville City map, Yashar aspired to learn how to build with the same level of detail, and his pyramid became the start point for Project Zearth.

# YASHAR'S TIPS

Players do not like empty, boring buildings, so make sure you create some beautiful interiors.

Connect built-up areas using roads and cover empty spaces with gardens and simple block decorations. The more you build, the more your city will take shape.

Varying the size of buildings and decorations is important. Try to build near a point of interest, such as a mountain or lake, and don't build on a flat world – try incorporating hills rather than removing them.

# SUBWAY

There's more to a city than what is visible. Beneath the ground there are sewage systems, and, of course, many cities have subways. Including a subway system in your Minecraft® city can really bring it to life, but the important thing is to know where you should put your subway stations. Make sure you have at least one in each corner of the map, although the size of the city will determine how many stations you'll ultimately need. It's vital not to place the subway too close to the surface or too deep – ten blocks down should be perfect.

## 1

## MATERIALS
Start by deciding which blocks you are going to use. You will probably want to use grey stone blocks, as you are constructing a subway underground and will want it to look solid.

## 2

## FOUNDATION
Start your main layer with two stripes of stone slabs. This is where the rails will go.

## 3

## FRAME
Frame the railway, marking where the rails are going and where your block level will be.

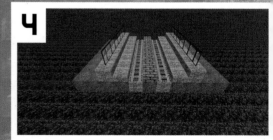

## 4

## RAILINGS
Place the rails and put fences alongside them so no one can jump onto them – you don't want any accidents!

## 5 WALKWAYS

Create walkways. This is not strictly necessary, but it does look good. It's also easy to make escape routes this way too.

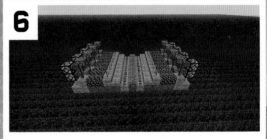

## 6 WALLS

Next, create walls. The decoration used here allows lighting into the tunnel, which looks great, but there are plenty of other options too.

## 7 ROOF

The height of the roof should not allow you to jump over the fence. Brick blocks look good when used for roofing.

## 8 LIGHTING

The lights at the sides aren't bright enough to illuminate the whole tunnel, so make a frame for ceiling lights to go in.

## 9

### CONNECT THE ROOF
Connect the roof with stone slabs, leaving spaces for redstone lamps.

## 10

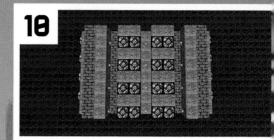

### REDSTONE LAMPS
Fill the empty spaces in the roof with redstone lamps.

# REDLIGHT CITY

**Shaders:** Chunky (Rendering Program)
**Point of interest:** Features a close
imitation of Sweden's tallest skyscraper,
the Turning Torso.

Redlight City is a heavily reworked piece of artificial
concrete made by just one person over a period of
three years. Around every corner you will find elements
from cities such as New York, Los Angeles, Berlin and
Stockholm. There are also numerous custom buildings,
skyscrapers, low-rise districts and industrial areas.

The city centre is divided into two downtown areas,
separated by Central Park. Both have tall New York–
inspired buildings at the tip of the skyline, with more
corporate skyscrapers adding horizontal layers to the
man-made mountain of steel.

The south centre lies towards the ocean, with several
docks providing access to the open sea.

The north centre is the heart of the oldest buildings
created and also home to the central subway station,
which reaches out under the city with three lines.

Outside the central area there are interesting places such
as an amusement park, an ancient and partly restored
fortified castle, and a train station with tall glass arches
that can be seen from afar and is the transfer point
for the subway and outgoing commuter trains. In the
corner, just behind the airport, you will find the film
studios, with different types of sets, including a motion-
capture stage and a couple of green-screen setups.

### THE BUILDER

Golonka – the builder behind Redlight City – was
encouraged to create a city after seeing some of the
amazing builds other players had created, although
he doubted he would be able to complete it by himself.
However, despite taking time off from the project every
now and then, Golonka stuck with it, and buildings
have been reworked, replaced or relocated constantly
as the game has been updated or he has become
dissatisfied with them.

# GOLONKA'S TIPS

Don't be afraid to remove your older buildings or simply reshape parts of them. This applies to anything that is heavily outdated or if you've changed your opinion on how it looks.

Experiencing cities and visiting your favourite real-life buildings is the best inspiration. You could make a replica, but it's better to integrate parts of what inspires you into your existing work.

# SIMBURBIA

**Download available:** www.jigarbov.net
**Time to build:** Eight months
**Unique builds:** 136
**Command blocks:** 58,000+
**Game time to complete:** 3–10+ hours
**Made for Minecraft version:** 1.8

The idea of Simburbia came about when Tim Gehrig was playing one of rsmalec's maps, called Tiny Minecraft®. This is a Minecraft game based loosely on the Tiny series on mobile platforms. In it, the player creates little houses and settings for villagers to live in. Tim found the tech used in the map interesting and could see it would be very easy to expand into bigger projects.

Tim's other inspiration came from *SimCity* by Maxis, and the idea to blend a *SimCity*-like experience in the world of Minecraft was a no-brainer. However, the amount of redstone, command blocks and logical prowess needed to craft Simburbia presented multiple challenges. Blending the tech of Tiny Minecraft, his own experiences with complex redstone, and new command block mechanics from version 1.8 of Minecraft, Tim was able to create his own version with the same meta experience players have come to expect from a modern-day city simulator.

Making it look like a city was also a challenge. Tim decided to utilise a 'macro style', where the buildings are much smaller than average house builds (these are buildings for your citizens, not for you). Making seamless roads, pathways and a power grid system was also tough to get right.

### THE BUILDER

Tim 'Jigarbov' Gehrig is 30 years old and works at the local cinema in his hometown of Edmonton, in Canada. In his spare time he creates worlds and is primarily an adventure map creator (see www.jigarbov. net). Using Minecraft, Tim infuses his builds with redstone and command blocks to bring them to life, often with assistance from his good friend Ron 'rsmalec' Smalec.

Tim has been playing Minecraft since the early Alpha versions of the game in 2011. He has created numerous popular maps, and his products have been downloaded more than 5 million times in total.

# TINY HOUSES

Building smaller than life isn't very common in Minecraft®, and it can be difficult to get good results. To start with, it is important to know your scale and to be consistent throughout.

A smart usage of stairs, half slabs and different blocks for accents such as doors and roofs is also crucial. Because everything in this macro style appears so small, you will need to be creative with the blocks you have. A log at a small scale could become a door, for example, while carpet is great for topping off your builds without creating much extra height.

So why not build a mini city on your favourite server and see your friends' reactions when they come stomping through the town streets below them!

## MACRO HOUSES
Place down your first macro houses, creating small 2x2x2 or larger 2x2x3 houses. Using different block types goes a long way towards making each house appear different, despite them being similar sizes.

## WINDOWS AND DOORS
Add windows and doors. Again, using different colours and materials can create very different results. Even using a slightly different-coloured wood plank on a wood plank house can give it a door effect.

## ROOFS
Don't forget the roof! Half slabs and carpet both make great roof tiles. You can also use special short blocks, such as the daylight sensors, which look great as both solar panels and whole roof coverings.

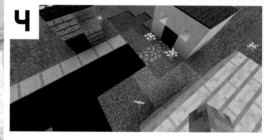

## TINY FINAL TOUCHES
Add finishing touches, such as roads, grass and gardens for your mini villagers. Don't forget footpaths and other tiny structures to really bring it to life.

# TIM'S TIPS

Simburbia uses a tile-based grid system for placing plots. With a system like this it is important that the edges blend to create a seamless and consistent look – having a common place where all the roads connect is a great way of achieving this.

Using a macro build style in Minecraft® is tough, because of the large size of the blocks. However, being consistent with your different building types and structures will go a long way towards creating a believable world at any scale. If you create just one building that looks out of place, it can take the player out of the experience.

Having a vision of the end product is paramount when designing ultra-interactive maps like this. Thinking about how players are going to interact with the world, how they will control the world and how they can traverse the world are all things you should know well in advance of actually implementing them.

# INTERACTIVITY

Having a tiny town to stomp around in is a lot of fun, but making it interactive is a whole other thing! The problem with adding details and hidden items is that they often stand out. Chests, dispensers, hoppers and other such things are so huge in this small town that it's important to add containers and buttons in a way that makes sense to your reduced scale.

When you build skyscrapers and other large (yet macro) buildings, the player is unable to go inside them. This means you can fill them with redstone and other command blocks to create some cool effects when the player interacts with them. Don't forget that the most important thing with containers is to name them appropriately.

## 1

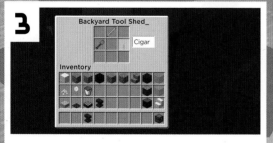

### CHESTS
An easy way to hide chests in macro builds is under half slabs. Chests can be opened, with stairs and half slabs above them leaving only small gaps.

## 2

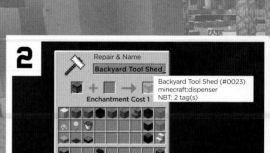

### BACKYARD TOOL SHED
Before you put a chest in your build, don't forget to name it with an anvil. This dispenser is named 'Backyard Tool Shed'.

## 3

### BACKYARD TOOL SHED ITEMS
Make a few items that you might find in a backyard shed. Screwdrivers, spades, old cigars . . .

## 4

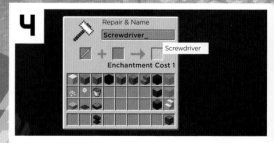

### ANVIL
Get an anvil and name them something different. This is a great way to add some personality to the items, especially as your items don't even need to be called what they actually are.

**5**

## COMMAND BLOCK

If you're using creative mode, get yourself a command block and name it.

**6**

## HIDING THE COMMAND BLOCK

Put the command block under the door of your little house so it's hidden from view.

**7**

Set Console Command for Block

Console Command

/say Hello, neighbor!

Use "@p" to target nearest player
Use "@p" to target random player
Use "@p" to target all players
Use "@p" to target all entities

Previous Output

– _____ 0

## MAKE A COMMAND

Right-click your command block and type in something like 'say Hello, neighbour!' and press Done.

**8**

## TOP IT OFF

Place a solid block with a pressure plate on top next to the command block. Now, when someone stands on it, it will be as if a tiny villager inside the house is talking to you.

# TWIN PEAK SKI RESORT

The idea of building a ski resort came to TheReawakens team after looking at Minecraft® builds and finding that no one had really made anything like it before. The team studied pictures of real ski resorts, laid out a base and began creating structures for it. Just as real resorts are designed around the ski slopes, so the Twin Peaks resort follows that notion as well.

The build features a tunnel leading through a mountain to the city, which has a variety of hotels, car parks and modern cars and machines. On the slopes there are chairlifts going to the top, slopes through the forest and a fun park for special skiing. It was difficult to put the build together, as it meant fitting in big hotels and having them connect to the slopes around the resort.

## THE BUILDERS

TheReawakens team includes members between the ages of 13 and 36 and a wide range of people working together. Most team members are from the United States and Europe, and spend a lot of time on their server making it a friendly environment and a welcoming place for new members and visitors. The team has a wide variety of build styles on its server, ranging from medieval to modern.

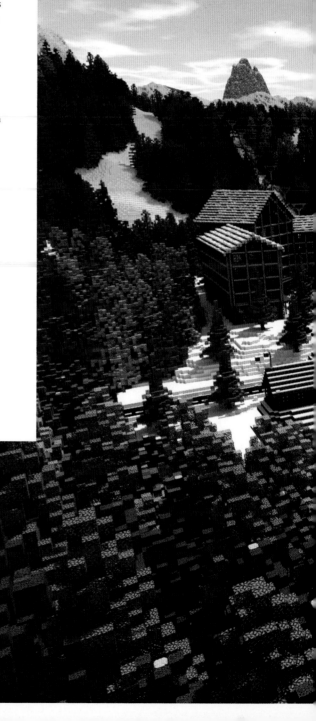

**Website:** www.reawakens.net
**Server:** TheReawakens
**Shaders:** Sonic Ether's
Unbelievable Shaders

**Mods:** Camera Studio
**Time to build:** 13 people,
12 hours

URBAN METROPOLISES

# LAMPPOST

Lampposts are a good item to fill out your city with and make it a little less plain. There are many variations that can be used for different areas of a city or different themes. The design shown here has a clean, modern look that suits both an alpine ski resort as well as a skyscraper city. Use wool for the body, as it gives a modern look with colour, and use slabs for the lamp, as it allows details to be added to the overhang.

### PILLAR
Make a white pillar four blocks tall and add two grey blocks of wool on top.

### PILLAR TOP
Add stone slabs in the pattern of a flat heart to the top of each pillar. Place one slab on top, two sticking out to the sides and a big one on the end with a small one beside it.

### EXPAND TOP FRAME
From the top of the frame, add an extra four-block extension to each side. Suspend an additional block under the third block.

### GLOWSTONE
In between the frame extension add two blocks of glowstone. You could switch the glowstone with beacons for another kind of lamp. You now have a fancy modern lamppost.

# SKI LIFT

Whether you want to create a small ski lodge or a whole city, you'll need a ski lift to transport players from the top to the bottom. Having the frame and foundation in place will help you plan the structure and interior design. Essential materials for this build will be wool or stained clay for a more metallic look. You should also consider where to build it in your city – try to connect it with another building for a cool look.

## 1

### FOUNDATION PILLARS

Start by making two pillars with a distance of 13 blocks between them. Add a small foundation around the pillars. The pillar at the front should be six blocks tall, and the one at the back three blocks tall.

## 2

### BUILD UP COLUMNS

Add a layer of stone brick on all sides of the columns. On the shorter rear column add a layer of stone slabs on top.

## 3

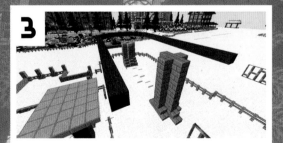

### FRAME

Add a frame for the structure around the top of the front pillar. There should be nine blocks of space between the sides and a half circle in the back.

## 4

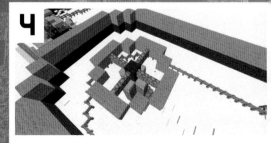

### WHEEL

On the back pillar, add a flat wheel to the top. Give it a diameter of seven blocks with a wool block at the centre and cobble walls connecting the circle. Add a layer on top of the frame.

## 5

### LINE THE FRAME

Add a couple of lines of wool on the front of the lift to simulate the entrances of the chain for the ski lift. There should be three blocks of space between each entrance.

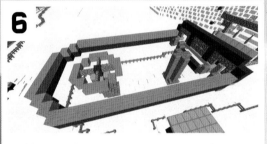

## 6

### WALL

Add cobble wall to the entrance. Leave an open spot at the centre of the two holes in the sides. Add a layer of stone slabs underneath.

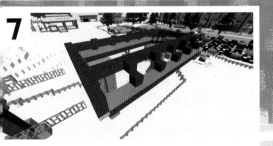

## 7

### BUILD UP FRAME

Add another frame on top of the existing frame. Make a three-block-wide space between each pillar connecting the frame. On the back make a five-block-wide hole at the centre.

## 8

### CHAINS

Have the chains go from the entrances made in the front to spin around the wheel in the back.

## 9

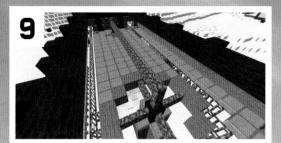

### FLOOR

Add a floor of stone slabs inside the lift so the whole area is filled out. Also add a line of cobble wall from the wheel to the front of the lift.

## 10

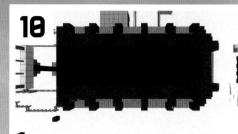

### ROOF

Fill in the top of the ski lift with a roof of grey wool. Two blocks in, add a new layer of black wool.

## 11

### WINDOWS

Add a layer of glass in each of the empty holes in the frame. You now have a functioning ski lift. You can try different colours for different slopes.

# THEREAWAKENS' TIPS

Never build fire in a winter landscape; it is much better suited to a desert or Nether kind of terrain.

Once you have your design ideas, start making them right away so they are fresh in your mind.

# CHAPTER 2

# FANTASY KINGDOMS

# ADAMANTIS

Adamantis is an enormous fantasy city built upon high cliffs from which natural springs and rivers flow, carried to the city by a network of aqueducts. The city's smaller buildings are built in tiers above the cliffs and are connected by walkways and bridges that lead to a large, open temple complex built into the highest cliffs, overlooking the city.

Although the arrangement and scale of the structures give a fantastical feel to the build, the project's style has its roots in the principles of classical architecture; the archways, colonnades and vaulted ceilings and domes found throughout the city follow classical principles of symmetry and proportion. The two vast colonnades that curve around the top of the entire city were inspired by the colossal Tuscan colonnades of St Peter's Basilica in Rome. The project is designed as a vertical build, with the city as tall as it is wide. The effect of the structures stacked on top of one another and towering above ground level creates a sense of awe.

### THE BUILDER

Having established one of the first professional build teams (the Mithrintia Build Team) in 2012, Jamdelaney1 went on to help set up BlockWorks with three other founders. As the managing director of BlockWorks, Jamdelaney1 is currently building full time during his gap year, but hopes to use his experience in design and construction within Minecraft® to study for an architecture degree. Adamantis is his solo project.

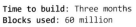

**Server:** Mithrintia Creative Server
**Mods:** WorldEdit, VoxelSniper

**Time to build:** Three months
**Blocks used:** 60 million

**FANTASY KINGDOMS**

**F**

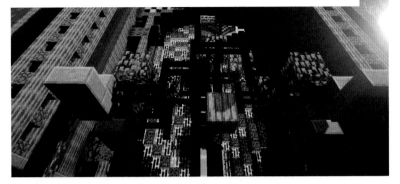

# CLASSICAL COLUMN

Classical columns feature in many different styles of architecture, and often help give structures a sophisticated and elegant look. This tutorial demonstrates how you can build a large column, but the principles can be applied to columns of any size.

**1**

## PROPORTIONS

Mark out the proportions of the column in three separate parts – the base (the bottom), the shaft (the middle) and the capital (the top). Different column styles have different-sized components.

**2**

## SHAPE

Mark out the width of each component. Both the base and capital should be wider than the shaft. Bases often taper up towards the shaft, while capitals spread out to meet the structure they're supporting.

**3**

## DETAILING

Classical architecture has a number of 'orders' (styles of column), but ornamentation is typically reserved for the capital, while the shaft and base are left fairly plain. More detailed columns will need to be larger to be fully effective.

**4**

## TEXTURE

Quartz is typically used for texture because of its pillar block, but stone can provide an equally effective finish.

# JAMDELANEY1'S TIPS

For a project the size of Adamantis, planning is essential. As soon as the plan was conceived for this build, the terrain and landscape upon which the city rests were the first elements to be developed. A building should always respond to its environment, and so the terrain should be completed before any structures are started.

Use odd measurements. This gives you the maximum potential for detail, as a centre block is maintained. For instance an arch between columns should span an odd number of blocks. This way the arch can have a point, or if it is a rounded arch, then its centre can be more easily and accurately detailed.

When building water features, use the invisible block (ID 36) to keep water from spilling. This is only possible with the use of mods/plugins such as WorldEdit or VoxelSniper.

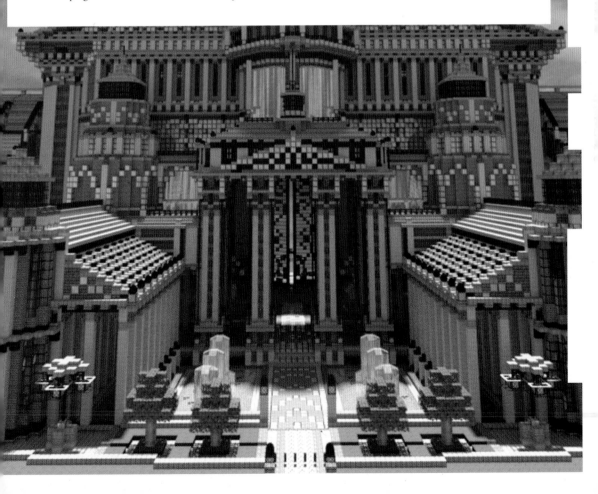

# CLASSICAL COLONNADE

The round, domed temple structures seen in Adamantis are among its standout features. They are classically styled with a circular colonnade and rounded archways.

## 1

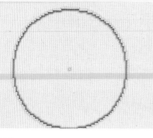

### DIAMETER

Mark out a circle with the diameter of the structure – this structure is 71 blocks in diameter.

## 2

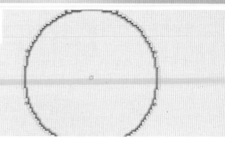

### COLUMN POSITION

Mark the locations of the columns, making sure they are evenly spaced. In this case eight columns were used.

## 3

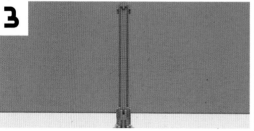

### FIRST COLUMN

Build a column, making sure its height is in proportion to the structure's diameter. Bear in mind that the height of the column is not the height of the final structure, as a dome will be added later.

## 4

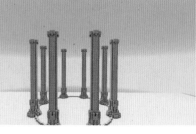

### MULTIPLE COLUMNS

Build a column on each evenly spaced mark. If you are using a mod/plugin such as WorldEdit, simply copy and paste the eight columns.

## 5

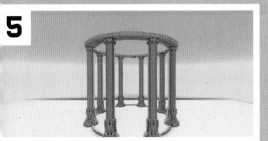

### ENTABLATURE

Build the entablature, which is the section that rests on top of the columns. This should be the same diameter as the first circle you marked out.

## 6

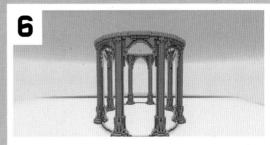

### ARCHES

Build arches between each column, making sure that the top of the arch lines up with the entablature.

## 7

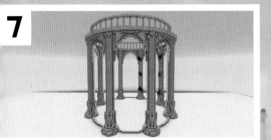

### SMALLER COLONNADE

On top of the entablature, build a second colonnade, this time with much smaller, one-block-wide columns. The columns should also be more frequent – in this instance three blocks apart. Build an entablature on top that the dome will rest on.

## 8

### DOME

Construct the dome. By far the easiest way to do this is to use a mod/plugin such as WorldEdit, which will automatically generate a perfect sphere of any specified diameter.

## 9

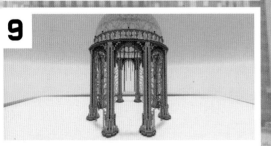

### TEXTURE AND DETAIL

Finally, add textures and details to the structure. For this example a blue and white palette was used – translucent blocks, such as ice and stained glass, are particularly effective for this style.

# THE VILLAGE— ADVENTURE MULTIPLEX 2

In the first Adventure Multiplex, the encounters that people built didn't have any real connection. The goal with this sequel was to create a cityscape with the plots of land that people submitted.

The main lesson learned from the original Adventure Multiplex was that it needed to be as simple as possible to import players' builds. Every contributor was given a basic template containing the ground and an entry point, with sample buildings and monument features provided for inspiration. This made it much easier to import each build, as all of the contributors were properly prepared.

The big question was what would this strange village look like? When looking at the overhead view of the town, it might appear haphazard, but each section in the village has builds in it that fall into specific groupings. Easy, Medium and Hard difficulties are separated, and each street is named to reflect the type of adventures that can be found in that area – Adventure Avenue and Parkour Place, for example.

### THE BUILDERS
Tim 'Jigarbov' Gehrig loves making maps. When he's not making them on his own, he's making them with groups of people – large groups of people.

Tim started the Jigarbov YouTube channel back in the early days of Minecraft®, with a simple video of him trying to get a zombie into a Minecart. Over time he decided to try to get his subscribers involved in building with him, which led to Adventure Multiplex, his first big map with community involvement. The project saw numerous people sending in templates to create a map of more than 80 different challenges in different categories.

Although Adventure Multiplex was a feat of engineering, people wanted more, so the call went out for Adventure Multiplex 2, which includes contributions from more than 70 players.

Download available: www.jigarbov.net
Time to build: Three months
Unique adventure encounters: 79
Maximum dimension of each encounter: 20x30x20
Game time to complete: 10-15+ hours
Made for Minecraft version: 1.7

FANTASY KINGDOMS

# GATING OFF AREAS

Creating a great adventure map requires a lot of time and effort. Not only will the players need to explore and interact with the environment you have created, but they also need to be motivated enough to continue through the adeventure world you've imagined. A good way to keep a player interested is by gating off certain areas, which can be unlocked at a later time or after completing a certain number of challenges so that a sequence and narrative is maintained. Gating has been used in games for a long time, and you can use this technique in your Minecraft® adventure maps.

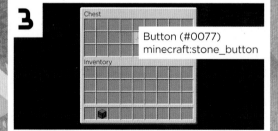

**1**

## WALL
First, you need to have two areas – one area that the player can get to and another they cannot. There are several ways to accomplish this, but for now let's just make a big wall.

**2**

## TNT BLOCK
Behind one of the blocks, put a single piece of TNT and a block of a different colour beside it so it looks important.

**3**

Chest

Button (#0077)
minecraft:stone_button

Inventory

## BUTTON
Once the player has completed the task you want, give them a button. In one of the houses at the end of the quest in The Village – Adventure Multiplex 2 you get this nice little button.

**4**

## BOOM
Instruct the player to put the button on the special block you specified. They press the button and BOOM, instant advancement!

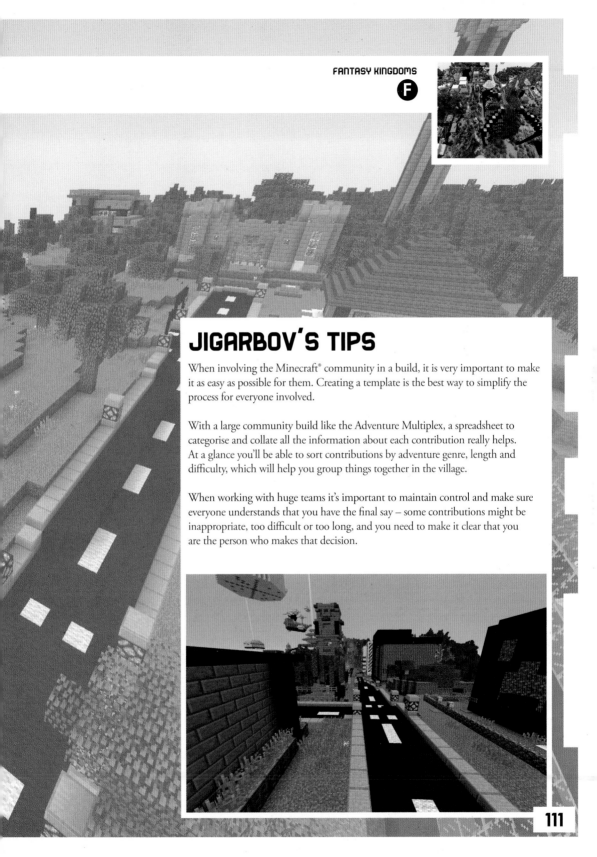

# JIGARBOV'S TIPS

When involving the Minecraft® community in a build, it is very important to make it as easy as possible for them. Creating a template is the best way to simplify the process for everyone involved.

With a large community build like the Adventure Multiplex, a spreadsheet to categorise and collate all the information about each contribution really helps. At a glance you'll be able to sort contributions by adventure genre, length and difficulty, which will help you group things together in the village.

When working with huge teams it's important to maintain control and make sure everyone understands that you have the final say – some contributions might be inappropriate, too difficult or too long, and you need to make it clear that you are the person who makes that decision.

# COMMANDS

Since the launch of version 1.8, there are myriad things you can do in Minecraft's creative mode using commands, from summoning scary monsters to cloning large bits of land and placing them right where you want. Commands are powerful and diverse and allow you to do things you could previously only achieve using mods.

The difference between commands and mods is that commands are part of the 'vanilla' game. This means you

don't need to modify your Minecraft client to use them – simply enter creative mode and you have all that power.

Adventure Multiplex 2 has a lot of commands that handle many of the map elements – from counting each encounter that you enter and complete to setting scoreboards within the adventure you're in. Commands can help tell a story and provide dialogue, although these only work in the PC version of Minecraft.

## 1 COMMAND BLOCK
Give yourself a command block using:
/give @p command block

## 2 COMMAND DIALOGUE
Place the command block where you want it, attach a button to it and right-click on it to open up the command dialogue. This will enable you to do some cool things with it.

## 3 SET COMMAND
Put this command in the command block and press done:
/summon Sheep ~ ~2 ~ {Riding:{id:Creeper, Riding:{id:PigZombie}}}

## 4 CREATURES
Now, when you press the button on the command block, you'll get yourself a strange stack of creatures!

# 1 SET COMMAND 2

Alternatively, try this command:
/give @p iron_sword 1 250
{display:{Name:Death Blade,Lore:["It will break on impact","destroying both blade and","foe. The Ultimate Weapon."]},ench:[{id:16,lvl:10}]}

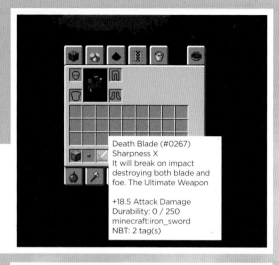

Death Blade (#0267)
Sharpness X
It will break on impact destroying both blade and foe. The Ultimate Weapon

+18.5 Attack Damage
Durability: 0 / 250
minecraft:iron_sword
NBT: 2 tag(s)

# 2 DEATH BLADE

Armed with the Death Blade, nobody will stand in your way! It will break both foe and blade on impact.

## F3 MODE

This one will be a bit more complicated. Press F3 and notice the targeting reticule has changed to three lines: one green, one red, one blue.

## FIND HOLE

Find a hole that you want to fill with water and stand at one corner with the reticule, as shown in the picture.

## SET COMMAND 3

Type the following and press enter:
/fill ~ ~-1 ~ ~-10 ~-4 ~-10 water 0 replace air

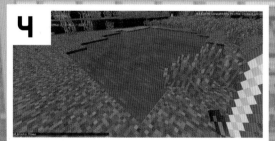

## FILL WATER

You just filled that hole with water! Commands are complex and powerful, so be careful.

# THE DESERT CITY OF ALAMUT

**YouTube channel:** www.youtube.com/user/anarrih
**Program used:** MCEdit
**Texture pack:** John Smith Legacy
**Time to build:** Two months
**Blocks used:** One million

The Desert City of Alamut was Luke Dargatz's first large-scale project. Inspired by the movie *Prince of Persia*, Luke became determined to build a desert city.

The first thing he constructed was the circular inner city, with the rest of the city designed around it. Working in Minecraft®'s creative mode, Luke used MCEdit to help with the build. Luke's original vision for the city was for it to appear abandoned and half buried in the sand, so exploring his map will uncover some buildings filled with sand, as well as an under city of buildings buried in the desert.

Luke's favourite element (and the last thing added to the build) is the giant dinosaur bones at the northern end of the city. These bones were originally built for another project but ended up in Alamut instead.

### THE BUILDER
Luke Dargatz is a 21-year-old human behavioural science student living in Canada. He volunteers his spare time to the Victims Assistance Unit of the local police department, with the intention of becoming a law-enforcement officer after completing his studies.

Luke's enthusiasm for Minecraft grew from his passion for art. While growing up, he liked to draw cartoons and eventually moved on to oil painting and pencil art. When he discovered Minecraft, it became his major creative outlet, enabling him to build fantasy and adventure realms that others could explore. This led to the creation of his YouTube channel, Anarrih's Minecraft.

Luke started as a lone builder, but over time came to work with other builders on large projects. He has now moved on from Minecraft to pursue other interests, but still enjoys seeing the creations of others and the amazing diversity of people's imaginations at work within the game.

# WATCHTOWER

Towers are a good addition to any ancient city. This tutorial will show you how to create a basic watchtower using easily accessible materials, but remember to experiment with materials to create a look that fits with your city. If you are building a castle city, try swapping the sandstone with stone bricks or cobblestone to get a more fitting look. Towers are also an easy way to wall off a city – simply build a number of towers around the perimeter and link them with walls. If you want to wall off a square-shaped area, build towers at each of the four corners, then connect the towers together. Add a gate at one side and you have a secured city!

## 1 BASE

Start with a circular base, leaving a space at the front for a door. For a different look, try using a contrasting block material for the floor.

## 2 SANDSTONE LAYERS

Add four additional layers of sandstone blocks on top of the base. After you place your door, you can fill the spaces above it.

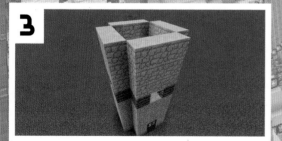

## 3 OAK LAYER

Add a layer of oak wood planks and glass for some windows. Do not put a window on the back wall. Add three more sandstone layers on top.

## 4 TOP FLOOR

Build the top floor out of oak planks, leaving an empty square on the back wall for a ladder. Add railings and supports for the roof using oak fences and posts.

## ROOF
Create a roof base using stone slabs, leaving a hole at the centre. Add two more layers to the top, making each layer smaller than the one preceding it.

## GLOWSTONE
Add a block of glowstone below the hole in the roof base. Finally, add a ladder on the back wall going from the floor to the roof.

# FREIGHTER SHIP

Ships are essential to any city built by water, as they add a sense of activity and give ports a thriving city feel. This tutorial shows you how to build a medium-sized, modern-style freighter ship utilising mostly quartz and wool blocks. If you want a more metallic look you can try using iron blocks, and if you want an older looking ship you can use wood or other more rustic materials (add a cabin and sails to create a pirate ship!).

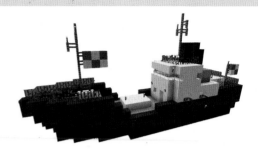

## 1

### BASE
Start with red and yellow wool. Build a 7x19-block rectangle with yellow wool at each end, one block away from the corners.

## 2

### SHAPE BASE
Add more yellow wool blocks directly above the first ones, then create a pointed bow and a rounded stern to the ship's base.

## 3

### LAYER BASE
Add one more layer of red wool to the base using the yellow wool as a guide. There should be some red blocks overhanging the bow and stern of the ship.

## 4

### DECK
Use blue wool to add another layer to the base. Fill in the central area with light grey wool to create the deck. The blue wool should overhang the bow and stern.

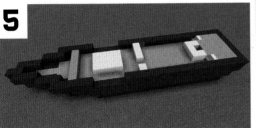

## LAYER DECK

Add another layer of blue wool, but this time only let it overhang the bow and leave a couple of gaps at the sides of the deck as well. Next, build up the base of the cabin.

## SHIP FRONT

Add two ascending (and overhanging) layers of blue wool to the bow of the ship. Build up the deck with light grey wool and add a couple of quartz blocks on top.

## LAYER CABIN

Add another layer of blocks to the cabin. Use blue wool for the back and quartz for the rest. Add some glass for windows and a few ladders both inside and out.

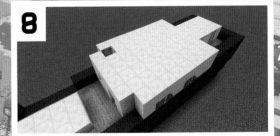

## CABIN ROOF

Add a cabin roof using quartz. Remember to leave a hole so you can access the cabin, and place ladders directly above the first ones.

## 9

### UPPER CABIN

Use quartz and glass blocks to build an upper cabin that is three blocks high and has a roof and windows. Do not build a back wall on the cabin at this point.

## 10

### CHIMNEY

Add a light grey wall of 3x5 blocks to the back of the upper cabin, then build a chimney stack on top using red and dark grey wool.

## 11

### ANTENNAS

Add various masts and flags to your ship using oak wood fences, white wool and cyan wool. Place redstone torches at the tops of the masts.

## 12

### DETAIL

Use iron bars to add railings to the stern, top and bow sections of the ship. Light the ship with torches, making sure that you place them where a ship's lights would be.

# LUKE'S TIPS

Not every idea you come up with will work out the way you first imagined it. Try experimenting with new building methods or find another way to make it come together. Remember, your build is a work in progress, so don't be afraid to incorporate new ideas.

Learn to use building assist programs such as MCEdit for large-scale builds. Utilising the programs available to you can speed up your build immensely, potentially saving you hundreds of hours of building time.

# ATROPOS

**Shaders:** Sonic Ether's Unbelievable
Shaders, RudoPlays Shaders
**Mods:** OptiFine, WorldEdit, VoxelSniper
**Time to build:** 120 hours
**Blocks used:** 4,081,921

Atropos is a mechanical tortoise with a city on his back.
The city is divided into three sections; the upper city, the
middle city and the lower city. The upper city consists of
the city's administration centre, which houses the city's
government: upside-down flying houses; and the light
catcher, which collects sunlight to provide power to the
turtle. The middle city contains the residential areas
and commercial district, as well as the city's fortress.
Finally, the lower city consists of more upside-down
houses, the hydro culture and the large engine room.
The hydro culture allows the city to be self-sufficient in
terms of produce, while the engine room houses four
colossal engines that allow the giant tortoise to move.
Exhaust fumes from the engines go out through the tail.

### THE BUILDER
Carlos is a 16-year-old from the Philippines. He
started building in Minecraft® using the single-player
commands mod (before there was a creative mode) and
enjoys large, mechanical builds. He prefers to build in
the steampunk, dieselpunk and sci-fi genres, inspired by
the work of artists Keith Thompson and Tsutomu Nihei
and the Warhammer 40,000 universe. He strives to
make his builds as efficient, detailed and memorable
as possible.

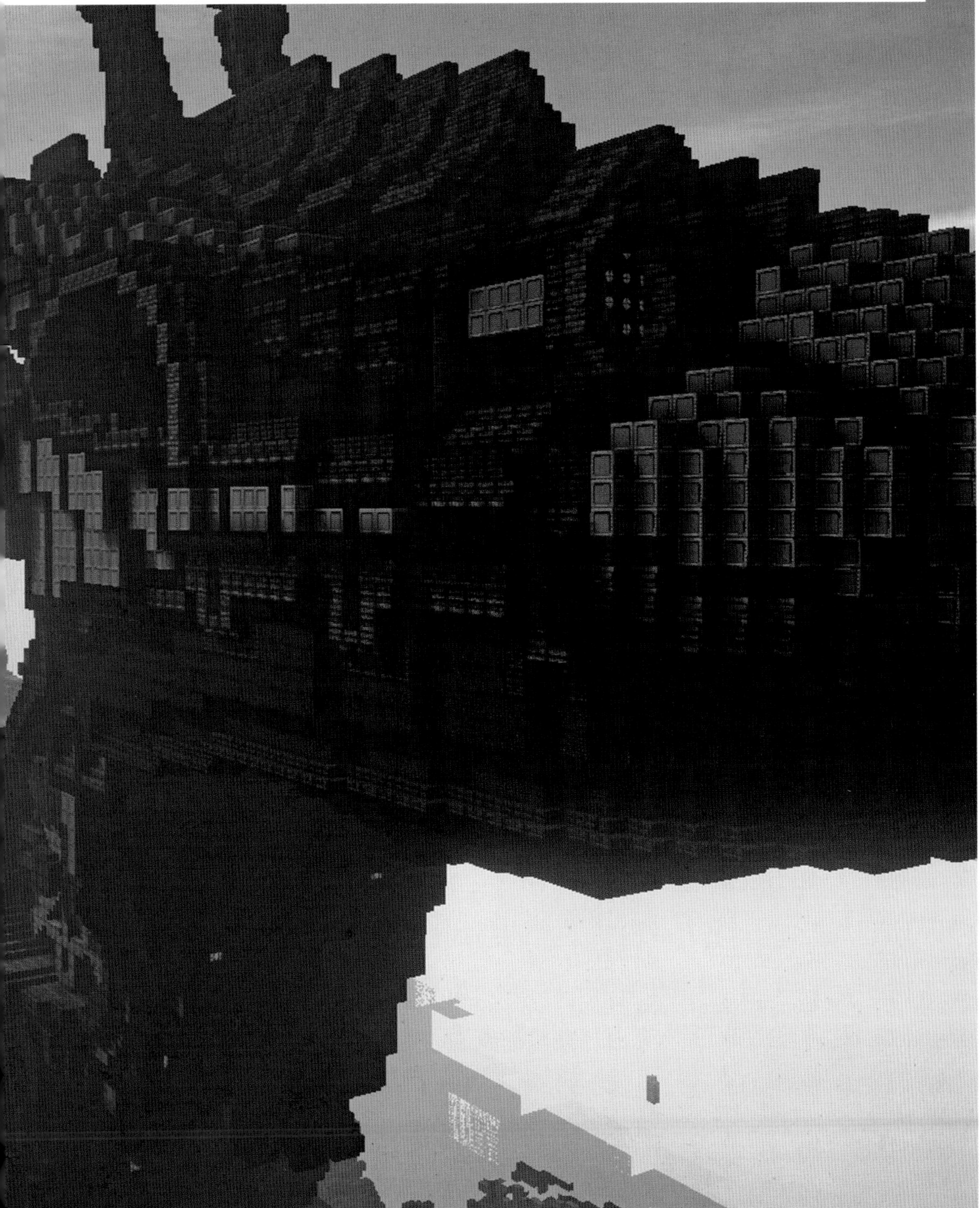

# CANNON

Cannons are a great way to give authority to your builds. You can put cannons on tanks, spaceships and fortresses. This basic tutorial can be used to create different styles of cannons. Follow the steps to get the basic shape and vary your materials to get the look you want.

## 1

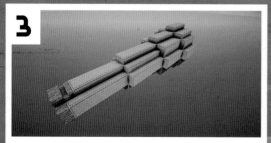

### TUBE

Start by making a tube. It can be made of wood, metal or stone, depending on the look you want, and in a variety of styles to evoke different eras.

## 2

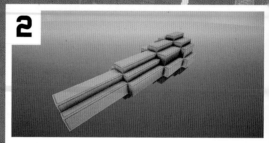

### SHAPE

Make the tube thicker as it gets closer to the back end.

## 3

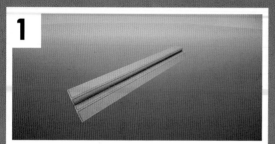

### MUZZLE

Create a muzzle for the cannon. The muzzle needs to be thicker than the tube. Again, the shape will help evoke the style – simpler shapes look more modern.

## 4

### FINISHING TOUCHES

Add reinforcement rings to each tier of the cannon, as well as some decorative details.

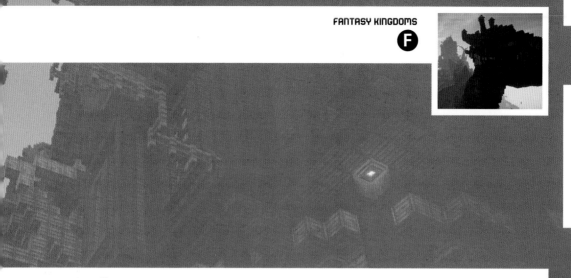

# CARLOS'S TIPS

Do not hesitate to use map-editing tools such as WorldEdit and VoxelSniper. I would be impressed if a logger felled a tree by punching it too, but the end product is the same, and the only difference between punching a tree and using a saw is the time wasted and the bloody hands. It is not practical to make large builds by hand if there are tools to assist you.

Have a plan, but don't stick to it too closely – it is important to have some degree of flexibility. No plan is perfect (no matter how painstakingly thought out it is), and having to adjust everything because of a slight discrepancy is frustrating.

# PIRATE ISLAND

**Texture pack:** John Smith
**Mods:** Anti-Grief Creeper
**Time to build:** One month

Pirate Island is an adventure map set in the Caribbean seas and stuffed with hidden treasures to find, including gold ingots, a compass and armour. The player must climb to enormous heights to reach the Lost Temple, but the map also features a prison, sewers, a smuggler's den that has a set of levers that must be pulled in the right order, cursed diamond mines and a voodoo village containing Black Beard's grave! While it is beautiful to look at, Pirate Island is designed with exploration in mind.

## THE BUILDER

Heaven Lord is from France and is an active member of building team Angel Block Society. He specialises in adventure maps, historic castles and fantasy worlds.

# HEAVEN'S TIPS

Medieval texture packs make it easier to build something with that theme.

Making a top-down plan on paper will help you to shape your design effectively, before re-creating it in Minecraft®.

Many buildings look better as asymmetrical structures. Creating outer walls on diagonal lines and placing windows on different sides of the building (and at different distances apart, while still aligned on the same floor) can make older buildings look more realistic.

# PYRAMID ADVENTURE

Pyramid Adventure was Jakpok Cooperative's first group project. The basic concept was to create an Indiana Jones type of adventure with a non-linear story and some interesting custom textures to give the map a distinctive look. The open-world concept meant that it was important to be able to predict player movement through the map, so random players were used as test subjects to plot their movements.

It took a full month to complete El Sharqi Village, and another month of work on the pyramid, which features three major battles and contains puzzles and parkour sections. Custom items such as a colt pistol, machete, camel milk and ammunition all play a role in the story.

### THE BUILDERS

Jakpok Cooperative is a team lead by Jakub 'Jakpok' Pokorski and Adam 'Haddock' Kawecki, with occasional help from friend Igor 'Niko' Jasik. The team members all come from the city of Toru, in Poland, and began playing Minecraft® together in its early days.

They also study at the same high school, which makes building together very easy, as they can discuss their various in-game tasks during break time. While Jakub and Igor study maths and science together, Adam is an art student. Because of his more artistic attitude and knowledge of architecture styles, Adam creates the concept art for the team's projects, as well as the map layouts and themes. Jakub does much of the scripting, modding and publishing of projects.

While Jakub plans to become a programmer and attend Gdańsk Technical University, Adam intends to gain a degree in arts and graphic design and move on to work in a video games studio. Their combined talents have helped them create some amazing Minecraft builds.

**Time to build:** Ten weeks
**Mods:** Custom resource pack
**Point of interest:** There are two hidden chests with Power Ranger outfits inside them somewhere in the map!

## JAKPOK'S TIPS

Use materials that fit the geology of the terrain you are re-creating.

Don't use Minecraft®'s default trees – build your own to create trees that are more suitable for your theme.

# VILLAGE HOUSE

The key to building an authentic-looking village is to perfect a simple hut or house. Keep the interiors cosy and rustic to maintain your realistic village theme. Use materials creatively to suggest details, such as ladders for vines.

## 1 FOUNDATION
Start with a floor shape and add one layer of foundation. Choose plain blocks for the floor itself and blocks with a visible pattern for the foundation.

## 2 WALLS
Build walls that are two blocks high, using blocks that are different from the foundation and that have a distinctive pattern. Make small holes and place glass panes in them.

## 3 INTERIOR
Remove some floor and place a colourful rug. Add some beds, fence dividing walls and two or three furnaces.

## 4 DETAILS
Add some ladders on a facade to imitate dried vines. You can also add some vertical fencing by the wall to imitate scaffolding and place wooden buttons at the top of each wall.

**5**

## GARDEN

Make a small garden with a simple bench made of wooden stairs, some dried shrubs and some ivy made of pine needles.

**6**

## FINISHING TOUCHES

A flat roof made of dark oak planks will contrast nicely with mono-coloured walls. You may also want to add some jungle leaves outside to make everything more vivid.

# VORPAL CITY

**Server:** Telcore Tradewinds
**Shaders:** Sonic Ether's Unbelievable Shaders
**Texture pack:** John Smith
**Mods:** Voxel build client, WorldEdit, VoxelSniper
**Time to build:** One month
**Point of interest:** Vorpal can successfully
house 200 players in roleplay, due to the
number of interiors.

Vorpal City was created for Minecraft® roleplay, with
the entire city designed around a strong storyline that
anyone can take part in.

> *Vorpal City, with its banner of 'Dream'*
> *flapping mutedly against the intricately*
> *carved architecture, looms tall in your*
> *visage. A comforting waft of the*
> *cityscape's white noise washes over*
> *your senses, enveloping you in the buzz*
> *and electricity of a city designed to be*
> *a monument to the achievements of*
> *the human race – and those that are*
> *to come.*
> **—John Larsen**

Built upon a dried-up lake bed, Vorpal City sits like a
beacon of hope and progress in the surrounding realm,
using its powerful steam technology to exact its grand
might over the populace. Yet Vorpal City harbours a
dark underbelly. Beneath the elaborate Upper City of
Vorpal sits a conflux of alleyways, dark streets and black
markets, where a dystopic atmosphere pervades.

### THE BUILDER
Joshua Haun is a 19-year-old 3D environmental artist
from California. Going by the handle Salmon77 in the
Minecraft community, Joshua switched from spending
hours playing Roller Coaster Tycoon to days playing
Minecraft in the early days of Minecraft's Alpha version.

He is primarily known for his steampunk and
Victorian builds, as well as his stunning CG renders
(he is currently involved in the CG industry for video
games and film, creating 3D environments). Joshua is
transfixed by the way builders take the blocky green
hills and haunted mines of Minecraft and turn them
into something never before seen. With Vorpal City,
the challenge was to transfer his Victorian steampunk
style into something believable in Minecraft.

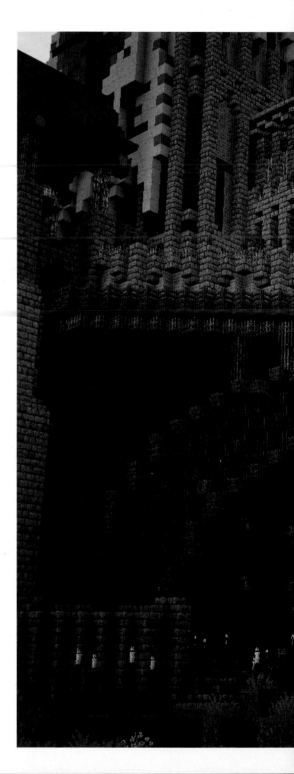

## JOSHUA'S TIPS

When constructing massive diagonal structures, such as Vorpal's arches, plotting out the element on grid paper can make the task less daunting and help you achieve greater accuracy.

A great way to achieve realism when designing and building cities is adding a sewer system. Vorpal contains an elaborate sewer system connecting many of the buildings together, which not only helps sell the scope of the city, but is also great for roleplay.

# PRINCIPLES OF DESIGN

Design plays a major role in virtually all Minecraft® projects: cities, organics, structures, and the natural environment all follow common principles of design.

This tutorial looks at a few design principles, which may seem daunting at first, but with practice they can become second nature.

## VISUAL PATHS

When designing in Minecraft it is a good idea to take into account how someone's eye will flow across your build. The detail in these elements suggests a path for the eye to follow. The implied lines formed by the textures of elements, along with the positioning of stairs, fences and logs, help create this path.

## EXAMPLE

This Victorian manor showcases the technique. By following the details of the structure your eye returns to the stained glass window at the centre.

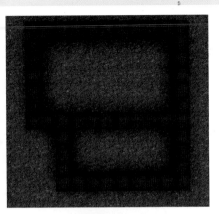

## THE GOLDEN RECTANGLE

The Golden Rectangle relates to the Golden Ratio, which was discovered in ancient Greece and found to have a visually pleasing quality. In simple terms, the Golden Rectangle suggests that space should not be distributed evenly, but instead follows a ratio where the rectangle is split in a way where one side is longer than the other. In this example, red wool has been laid out so that the extruded side is longer than the other, thus following the Golden Rectangle and creating some visual interest.

## EXAMPLE

The Golden Rectangle doesn't only suit floorplans; it can be used to divide many structures or compositions. Here, a structure in Vorpal City is divided in a way that uses the ideology behind the Golden Rectangle.

## USING COLOUR

Colour theory plays an important role in bringing a sense of mood to your creations. Colour harmony can be achieved in many ways, including the use of contrasting colours such as red and green, or orange and blue. Here, red wool accents the sandstone wall.

## EXAMPLE

The red stools in this interior bring a sense of life to the hall that makes you feel more immersed in the environment. For colour contrast, green bottles have been added.

Before complexity pass        After complexity pass

## VISUAL INTEREST

How much visual interest does your build have? Too much detail can be an eyesore, while not enough can leave the viewer unimpressed. It's common to use trapdoors, fences and stairs to make builds appear more complex. This example utilises pushed and pulled flat stone wall to create a sense of depth. If your builds feel too simple, find areas that lack detail and push and pull on these elements until you're happy with them.

## SCENERY DETAIL

Trees, terrain, props and figures can all add detail to your build, creating a visually pleasing composition. However, try to avoid overpowering your scene with too much content.

## SYMMETRY

Symmetry was used extensively by ancient Greek and Roman architects. If you were to draw a line down the middle of a symmetrical building, both sides would appear the same. This can be achieved easily in Minecraft® by using the WorldEdit flip and rotate commands.

Symmetry can also exist in a circle when elements are laid out radially – with gazebos and dome extrusions, for example.

You can also utilise asymmetry (a lack of symmetry) to make your builds uneven and promote the idea of chaos and disorder.

## CITY PLANNING

In the design of Vorpal City, the first decision was how the city would be laid out. This involved asking questions, such as how people would get around – would they use roads, trams or boats – and what activities would the city house?

Asking yourself questions when you are planning a build is a great way to get the project started, and it can also make it easier to transition into the building stage. You might also want to try to draw a map that demonstrates how your city might work – this will make the challenge of building your city much

## NATURAL CITIES

You rarely see flat cities, and it is the changing elevations in the lower section of Vorpal that help create both realism and complexity.

Cities are also not built by a single architect. They are the work of different people over centuries, so there should be a variety of styles at play in your build to reflect this.

Finally, cities are like rainforests. In canopied forests plants often compete for the little sunlight there is, growing over and around each other just to get a taste of the light. In cities, buildings do the same thing, although they aren't competing for the sun, they are competing for your attention.

# YATHERIN PALACE

**Server**: TheReawakens
**Shaders**: Sonic Ether's Unbelievable Shaders
**Mods**: Camera Studio
**Time to build**: One month
**Blocks used**: Quartz, lapis, gold, stone brick, stone slabs, leaves, ice, water

With Yatherin Palace, builder Daniel Thage's aim was to create a magical kind of city. Built as a single, giant structure, the palace is located on a large cliff at the centre of a mountain range. A huge bridge connects the mountains to the palace and is the only entry point from the mainland to the cliff. The palace is made up of towers and a large housing area, which are positioned around a central throne tower. Daniel's favourite element of the city is the way that the white walls flow together – the use of ice for windows helps maintain this flow.

### THE BUILDER

Daniel Thage is a 19-year-old engineering student from Denmark and a member of TheReawakens Minecraft® team. Daniel spends a lot of his day securing and running the team's server community and coming up with fantasy build ideas, but when he is building, his main motivation is to challenge himself and push the limits of his skills. In pursuit of this he builds in every kind of genre, from medieval to futuristic.

## DANIEL'S TIPS

Don't overestimate what you can build.
Starting a project that is too big might
prevent you from finishing it.

Work with materials that fit together.
Experiment with different blocks and
pick the ones that have the best match.

Don't make totally symmetrical builds.
Experiment and add little extras to different
parts of the map to make it unique.

# ICE GATE

When making a castle, palace or fantasy-style city, you'll need a castle wall around it and a gate for people to get in and out of the city. Your gate should be epic in scale, so that people coming to your city will know from just the gate how awesome it is! This tutorial will guide you in building a magical, icy gate.

## 1

## FRAME
Start by making a frame for the gate doors. Each door of the gate should be 18 blocks tall and 6 blocks wide, with a steep curve at the top – together the two doors will form a formidable entrance.

## 2

## HINGES
Connect each door to the wall by making small hinges on the inside of the open gate using iron fence. Include a small separation in each hinge.

## 3

## LAYER
Add a layer of stone slabs along the inside edges of each gate door with a horizontal row of slabs running across the centre.

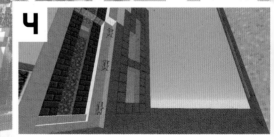

## 4

## FILLER
Fill the remainder of each gate door with packed ice to make it solid. You can use different materials, depending on how solid you want your gate to appear.

## 5

## HOOKS

At the centre of the gate doors, add three trip-wire hooks at each side to represent the place you put a board to keep the gate closed.

## 6

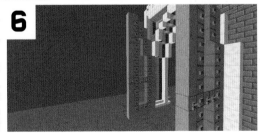

## SURFACE DETAIL

On the rest of the stone slabs, fill in the surfaces with buttons to give the appearance of screws sticking out of the gate.

# CITY WALL

A wall will help keep uninvited people out of your city. Always start by laying the foundation on the ground, and then stack up the wall so you can get an idea of the length and height of it. This will help you visualise whether it will match the size of your city. Essential materials will be any kind of stone, wood or quartz for the solid part of the wall, but it is important to make sure the wall matches the materials used for the rest of your city.

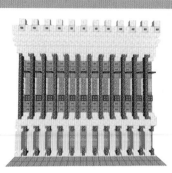

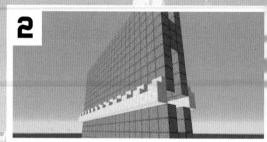

**1**

### WALL FRAME
Start by laying out two lines of double stone slabs. Make the lines 24 slabs long, separated by one block of air. Stack up the wall so it is 17 blocks high from base to top.

**2**

### QUARTZ
On each side of the wall, add a line of quartz blocks, five blocks from the base of the wall. Add a quartz stair on top of every second block, making sure it is symmetrical on both sides of the wall.

**3**

### ICE AND GLOWSTONE
Three blocks from the top of the line of quartz stairs add a three-block-tall layer of packed ice and gold blocks. The ice should align with the quartz stairs added in the previous step. Add a glowstone behind each of the ice blocks.

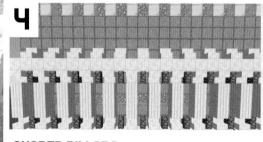

**4**

### QUARTZ PILLARS
At the base of the wall you need a foundation. Every second block of the wall should have a quartz pillar, with a stair at the top and bottom. Add a cobblestone wall in the space between the pillars.

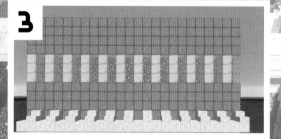

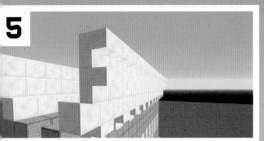

## 5

## TOP LAYERS

At the top of the wall, add three layers of quartz. The bottom layer should be a quartz block, and the two upper layers should be quartz stairs. The quartz block should be on the outside of the wall, and the stairs should be outside the block.

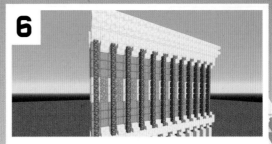

## 6

## COBBLESTONE WALL

Between the top and bottom stairs, add lines of cobblestone wall. These should rise up from the quartz pillars to the top of the wall. Make sure they are placed on top of the gold and not the packed ice.

## 7

## QUARTZ AND GOLD

At the top of the wall, add a layer of alternating quartz and gold blocks. On top of the gold blocks, add a quartz stair, and on the outside of the gold block, add a wooden button.

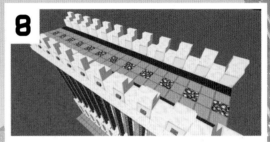

## 8

## WALL FLOOR

In between the top crenellated walls add the floor; red wool at the sides and stone slabs at the centre. Place glowstone blocks in the floor for light, which will give a good effect at night.

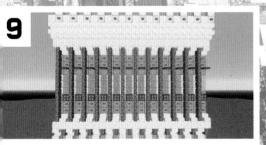

## 9

## FINISHING TOUCHES

On the side of the wall, add a mix of buttons and trapdoors. The trapdoors should be placed just above and below the ice, with buttons added to the remaining flat blocks.

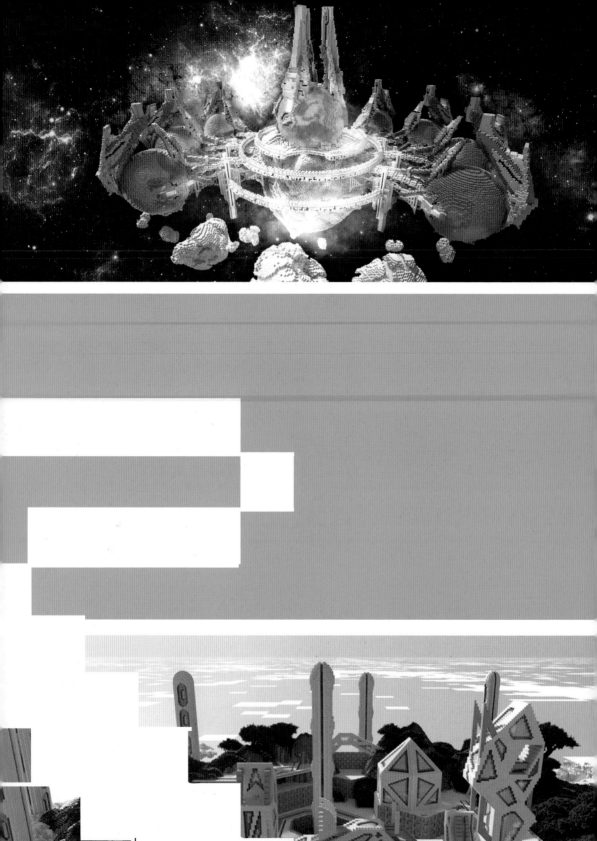

# CHAPTER 3

# FUTURISTIC ZONES

# AETERNIUM

Floating high above the earth exists a vast fantasy dream world, full of strange and extraordinary mechanical creatures. Clockwork bumblebees fly among the mountains, while a mechanised turkey grazes below. At the centre of this dream world is a steam-powered orchestra. Huge, complex contraptions operate a wide variety of instruments, which perform in synchrony as one melodic collective: the Symphony of Dreams.

Having decided to pursue a project in a steampunk style, a musical theme seemed ideal, as it allowed the builders to assemble instruments such as bells, horns and pipes, which represent the steam-powered mechanisms of the style. The overall plan was drawn up as a huge theatre complex, with the instrumental components fixed around the central theatre area, including an organ, violin, harp, trombone, percussion, saxophone, guitar and contrabassoon. As a finishing touch it was decided to adapt the full landscape of the island upon which the main structure was built, adding mechanised creatures throughout.

### THE BUILDERS

BlockWorks is a large team of designers, architects and animators working within Minecraft®. There are between 20 and 30 builders on the team at any one time, who often work in partnership with other builders and map-makers for specific projects. Aeternium was created by 13 members of the team.

BlockWorks is a truly international team, with members from New Zealand, America and Europe, and with a wide age range of 13 to 32 years. Within this diversity, however, is a unifying fascination and love of the creative potential of Minecraft – whether it be the opportunity to create fantasy dreamscapes or sprawling metropolises. While the team completes commissioned work on a regular basis, Minecraft is valued as an artistic medium among the builders.

BlockWorks does not build in any signature style, aiming to recruit members skilled in different themes to broaden its creative scope. It does, however, value the importance of shaping and form and considers this above all else to be the essence of any great build.

**Server:** BlockWorks team server (private)
**Shaders:** Sonic Ether's Unbelievable Shaders

**Mods:** WorldEdit, VoxelSniper
**Time to build:** 5.5 days
**Blocks used:** 17,524,761

**FUTURISTIC ZONES**

# STEAMPUNK GEAR

A key characteristic of the steampunk style is mechanical features such as cogs or gears. On their own they appear static, but when a number of these components are brought together the impression is made of moving and working machinery. This is a basic cog wheel; the techniques used can be applied to gears and cogs of any size.

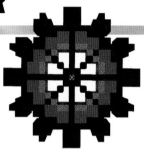

## 1

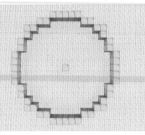

### FRAME
Determine the centre point of the cog, then build a basic circle around that centre, with whatever radius you want the cog to have. This can be most easily done using Minecraft® circle charts or mods such as WorldEdit, which have circle generator functions.

## 2

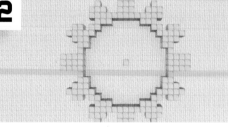

### TEETH
Around the outside of the circle, add the cog's teeth, evenly spacing protrusions from the circle. The number of teeth you add is up to you, but multiples of four tend to work best.

## 3

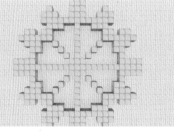

### SPOKES
Add spokes to the cog if you want to make it partly transparent. Alternatively, fill the circle in for a more solid-looking wheel.

## 4

### TEXTURE
Finally, add textures and additional details to suit the theme you are attempting. This example utilises warm brown and red colours, but for a more industrial look you could use darker grey textures instead.

# BLOCKWORKS' TIPS

When you are working on a large-scale project it is important to have an element of continuity running throughout the build. In this case, the distinctive palette of brown/red hues, as well as mechanised detailing, is the connecting motif.

Minecraft® has no set scale, so play around with the size of objects to achieve interesting effects. This project includes huge musical instruments, the details of which could be interpreted as the details of a vast fantasy city.

The best builds always respond to their environment. The fantasy theme of the structure connects to the cloud-based terrain to give a dream-like atmosphere. The build is largely abstract and something that could perhaps only ever exist in a dream state.

# VIOLIN

One of the many instruments included in Aeternium is a violin. The basic method of construction for this and many of the other instruments is to first measure and outline the shape before adding details and texturing the build.

## 1

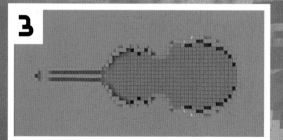


### FRAME

Mark out the shape of the violin's main body. This is the most difficult stage and it is worth spending time to make sure the shape is as accurate as possible. Do not worry about texture or detail yet.

## 2

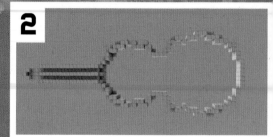

### NECK

Above the body, mark out the shape of the neck – there should be a subtle tapering towards the top of the neck.

## 3

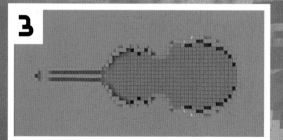

### BODY

Fill the main body of the violin using a different texture to the outline.

## 4

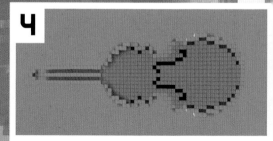

### F-HOLES

Add two 'F-holes' to the violin's body; these should be one block deep.

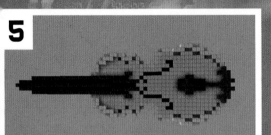

## 5 LAYER

Extend the neck so it comes down onto the top part of the violin. At the same time, build a tailpiece near the bottom. The violin strings will stretch from the top of the tailpiece to the top of the neck.

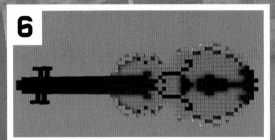

## 6 BRIDGE

Add the bridge. This should be in the middle of the two F-holes, between the neck and tailpiece. Add the peg box at the top of the neck. This is characterised by a scroll at the top and four tuning pegs, two at either side of the peg box.

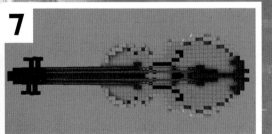

## 7 STRINGS

The strings are placed next to each other. You need to use both cobblestone wall and wooden fences so that the strings do not connect sideways.

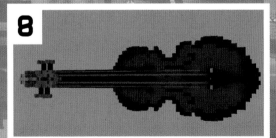

## 8 TEXTURE

Retexture the violin appropriately, taking the opportunity to add some finer details to the peg box. Use stairs and slabs to make a more defined scroll shape, and stairs to suggest the turning potential of the tuning pegs.

# ANDROMEDA

**Server:** BlockWorks team server (private)
**Shaders:** Sonic Ether's Unbelievable Shaders
**Mods:** WorldEdit, VoxelSniper
**Time to build:** One month
**Blocks used:** 886,689

This *Halo*-inspired futuristic build successfully exudes the awe and amazement that is a defining feature of the science-fiction aesthetic. While appearing highly technical, the mechanics and infrastructure look entirely alien due to the organic and naturalistic forms that run throughout the build.

Andromeda consists of a space station attached to a large meteorite. At the centre of the build is a gravity well, a piece of alien technology common to the *Halo* games. Surrounding the well are seven capsule sections of the space station. Finally, extruding from the bottom of the meteorite are two landing bays, which provide access into the station's central structure.

This was a particularly difficult build to pull off. Although the team wanted a futuristic feel, they didn't want it to feel human in any way. The aesthetics of both the *Halo* and *Alien* franchises are heavily influenced by the work of sci-fi surrealist, H. R. Giger. For this project, that meant shaping was absolutely essential for the successful creation of a truly 'alien' space station. Consequently, more time was spent perfecting the shape of the project than on the detailing or any other aspect of the build.

### THE BUILDER
As one of the original founders of BlockWorks, Block_Fortress has been one of the most influential figures in the creative community since Minecraft®'s beginnings. Currently undertaking a physics degree in New Zealand, Block successfully juggles a busy schedule of studying and building to an extremely high level. His ability to conceptualise and form complex 3D shapes in Minecraft gives all of his builds an impressively simple visual effect. Block's builds do not require complex or dense details – the forms of his designs are interesting enough on their own.

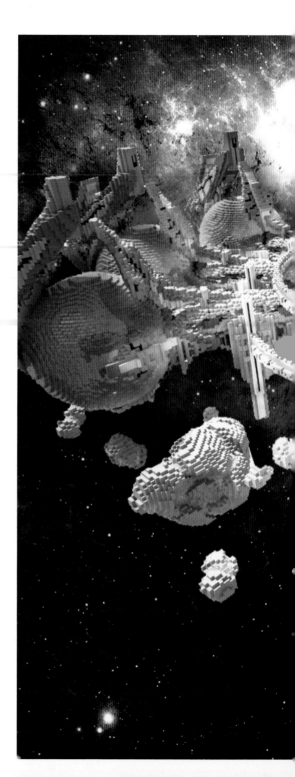

# BLOCK'S TIPS

The use of transparent and translucent textures, such as ice and stained glass, is particularly helpful in creating an alien theme. Translucent textures help give the impression of force fields and energy shields.

This build uses repeated segments positioned at different angles. On a large project such as this, it is worth investigating the relevant tools within the WorldEdit and VoxelSniper plugins that allow you to rotate entire sections to custom angles. This will save you a lot of time.

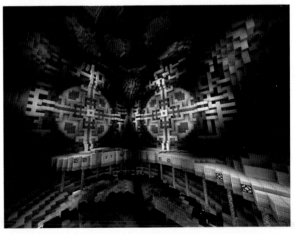

# CLOUDHAVEN

One of the great things about Minecraft® is that real-world physics don't apply: if you want to create a giant floating city that weighs 50,000 tons and runs on steam power, you can.

The lore envisioned for Cloudhaven is that of a post-apocalyptic world, but the apocalypse doesn't have to be all doom and gloom! While most dystopian futures are buried beneath an endless sea of grey cloud, Cloudhaven rises above, like a ghostly galleon tossed upon cloudy seas.

The city was imagined as an airship built for mining the surrounding floating islands for Kohi' Noor crystals, which enable its lighter-than-air flight. However, after a void storm destroyed the surface of the planet, Cloudhaven was left to fend for itself. One hundred years later and it is now a sprawling mass of wooden walkways, towers and homes, with the descendants of the original survivors eking out a living in cramped spaces, with houses climbing on top of each other to feel the warmth of the sun.

The giant city-ship is surrounded by enormous, shattered floating islands, which are trapped in a circular orbit due to the gravitational pull from the ship's engine.

## THE BUILDER

Dan Lynch first started playing Minecraft in 2010, after coming across some videos of the game on YouTube. For Dan, Minecraft represents one of the greatest games of his generation – one that sparks the imagination, challenges players and can create a safe environment online to play with friends and work together to build mind-boggling creations.

Dan's biggest influence comes from Studio Ghibli movies, such as *Howl's Moving Castle* and *Spirited Away*. The sense of solitude and otherworldliness encapsulated in these movies fuels ideas that Dan can make solid in Minecraft.

**Server:** Telcore Tradewinds
**Shaders:** Sonic Ether's
Unbelievable Shaders
**Mods:** WorldEdit

**Time to build:** Three weeks
**Blocks used:** Cloudhaven is more than
300 blocks long and 200 blocks high

FUTURISTIC ZONES

# CLOCKTOWER

Clocks and clockwork items are a major feature of any steampunk build. Creating a clocktower is reasonably straightforward, but the more of them you make, the more unusual features and details you can incorporate.

## FOUNDATION
Create four stacks of logs, seven blocks high. Leave five blocks of space between each stack.

## WALLS
Create walls connecting the stacks on the inside using wooden planks.

## LAYER BASE
Add logs to connect the tops of the stacks, glowstone blocks on top of the planks to let some light inside, and wooden fencing on top of the logs.

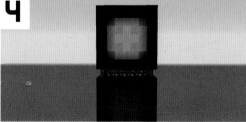

## CLOCK FACE
Build the clock face frame using logs. Make the clock face using light grey wool, white wool and snow blocks.

## 5

### CLOCK HANDS
The clock hands and numerals can be made using a fired piston, fence post, fence gate and wooden buttons.

## 6

### SHAPE AND LAYER
Place wooden stair blocks to curve the face of the clock. Add a line of wooden planks on top, in preparation for the next step.

## 7

### ORNATE FRAME
Place stair blocks all around the clock tower at the top and below the clock face to create an ornate frame. Use fence posts at the corners to make slim pillars.

## 8

### LAYER ROOF
Lay down the first layer of the roof using wooden planks.

## 9

**LAYER ROOF**

Add a second layer using wooden planks and stair blocks.

## 10

**LAYER ROOF**

Add a third, narrower layer.

## 11

**LAYER ROOF**

Add a final layer and a fence post spike on top.

## 12

**ROOF DETAIL**

Place fence posts and wooden half slabs at the corners of each roof stage.

## 13

**ROOF DETAIL**

Stair blocks placed upright and upside down can add depth to your roof.

## 14

**FINISHING TOUCHES**

You can change the height of your base to customise your build.

## DAN'S TIPS

Symmetrical builds tend to look best, because the brain likes order! Try to make each side of a build have similar proportions, so if you were to cut your build in half and hold a mirror up to it, each side would look the same.

Put together a selection of inspirational material, whether it's images, video, books or music. Remember, you are what you eat, and the more interesting things you feed your brain, the bigger the supply of inspiration there will be to fuel your fantastic Minecraft® creations.

# TUDOR-STYLE HOUSE

There are countless styles you could use to build a house for your city in Minecraft®. Tudor houses use very specific materials to get their look, which works equally well in both medieval and steampunk cities and villages.

### 1

**FOUNDATION**
Place down six stacks of logs, three blocks high. Separate the stacks by three blocks each.

### 2

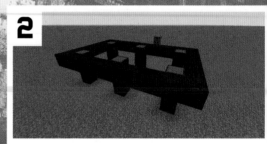

**FOUNDATION PILLARS**
Place another set of logs around the outside of the foundation pillars.

### 3

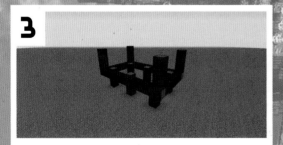

**FRAME**
Place four stacks of logs, three blocks high, at each corner.

### 4

**ROOF OUTLINE**
Create a roof outline using logs.

## 5

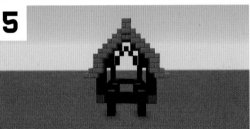

### LAYER ROOF

Create a roof outline with stone stairs and stone blocks on top of the wooden outline. Extend the roof out one block further than the wooden blocks. Add depth to your roof by using upside-down stair blocks.

## 6

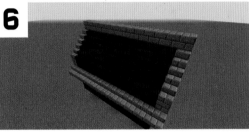

### FILL ROOF

Place a line of stair blocks around the top and bottom edges of the roof to create a framework. Fill the inside section of the stone frame using wooden stairs and wooden planks.

## 7

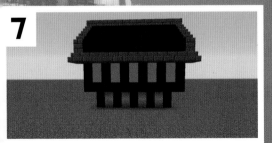

### WALL DETAIL

Create Tudor-style walls using white clay, wool and logs.

## 8

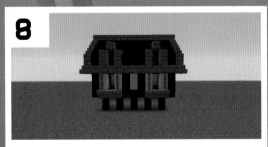

### WINDOWS

Add windows to allow some light in.

## 9

**STAIRWAY**

Use stone bricks to create a stairway that extends three blocks out from the ground floor. Add stairs.

## 10

**HANDRAIL**

Add a fence post handrail for decoration.

## 11

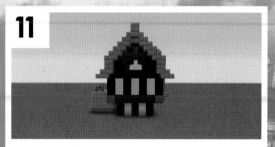

**DETAIL**

Decorate the front and back of the house by adding a top window and creating Tudor-style walls, as detailed in step 7.

## 12

**END WINDOW**

Include a window for more decoration.

## 13

**ROOF DETAIL**

Give the roof a more interesting shape by using half slabs and stair blocks.

## 14

**CHIMNEY**

Add a decorative chimney using stone buttons, stone bricks, stone stairs and cobblestone fence, plus cobwebs for smoke.

# FORGEHEART

**Server:** Sanacraft (sanacraft.mcfrag.net:25665 /
http://www.planetminecraft.com/server/sanacraft/)
**Mods:** WorldEdit and VoxelSniper
**Time to build:** Ongoing from 2013

Forgeheart was planned as a massive and mostly
realistic-looking steampunk city, surrounded by several
smaller settlements connected by train tracks and roads.
The buildings and machinery have been crafted to be
as detailed and realistic as possible, to produce one of
the all-time great Minecraft® projects.

While the settlements are designed primarily as a
training ground for newer players, Forgeheart itself
is a carefully planned city where only the most skilled
players are allowed to build. This became necessary to
maintain control of the growth of the city and make
sure the theme and style stay consistent throughout.

One of Tobias's favourite spots is the East Plaza, a
beautiful place of inspiration and art made by two
amazing builders, chappedlips and letsmeetjesus,
both members of the Sanacraft admin team.

While the builders are nowhere near finished working
on Forgeheart, some areas can be considered complete,
giving an impression of how the finished city will one
day look.

### THE BUILDERS
Tobias Wolfbeiß is a 31-year-old from Germany and a
gamer to the core. He was immediately hooked when he
discovered Minecraft in 2011, and within a few months
he had created the Sanacraft server and started his first
mega-project, an ancient city. More and more skilled
builders joined the server, and eventually the Forgeheart
project began.

Sanacraft is quite a mature server, but younger players
are also welcomed. The majority of the team is from the
United States, although there are also members from all
around the world. Sanacraft is still a small and relatively
unknown team, but its ambition is to establish itself as
one of the biggest creative building servers.

# WATERWHEEL

If you are a fan of steampunk, you will likely want to make mechanical objects at some point, and nothing is better for that than large gears. They can be used in all kinds of machinery and can also serve as a simple waterwheel.

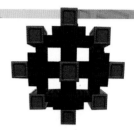

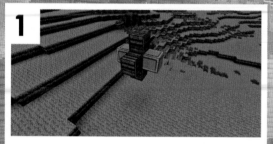

## 1

### AXIS
Make the axis of the gear from three iron blocks. Add a wooden block at the centre of each side of the axis.

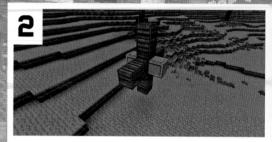

## 2

### LAYER
Add another wooden block to the wooden blocks placed in step 1.

## 3

### STAIRS
Add wooden stairs at every side. You may need to move below the structure so the stairs will attach correctly to the wooden blocks.

## 4

### IRON BLOCKS
Add iron blocks at even intervals all around the gear. They will fit perfectly into the gaps between the stairs.

# TOBIAS'S TIPS

Before you start building, use a colourful block such as wool to outline the dimensions of your build. Make sure you know the shape and size of your buildings and where entrances and other special features will go. Use the wool as a means of sketching your building.

No matter what you plan to build, there are probably blueprints of them available on the web. If you're trying to build something as realistic-looking as possible, study blueprints and floorplans before starting a new project.

Detailing your building is important if you want a good-looking project, but overdoing it can produce the opposite effect! A plain wall may not look great, but neither does a wall overloaded with different things. Moderation is the key.

# STEAMPUNK HOUSE

This tutorial shows you how to make a small wooden house with the addition of some cobblestone and clay. It works well in a small- or medium-sized town, or on the outskirts of large cities. While originally designed for a steampunk-themed world it could also fit into a medieval build as well. By modifying the base of the building you can give it the shape or size you want.

## 1

### FOUNDATION
Outline the base of the building with cobblestone. Keep gaps of three blocks between the blocks so windows will fit in later.

## 2

### BASE
Stack logs on top of the cobblestone blocks and then fill in the cobblestone base outline.

## 3

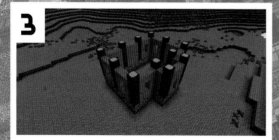

### FILL
Use clay to fill the gaps between the logs, leaving openings for the windows and the door. No window is needed at the back of the building, as a chimney will be placed there.

## 4

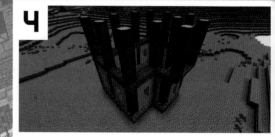

### LAYER
Add a row of wood on top of what you have created so far and start stacking logs again. Above the door, use stair blocks to make a small overhang.

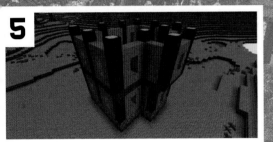

## 5

## FILL

Fill the gaps with clay again, remembering to leave openings for the windows.

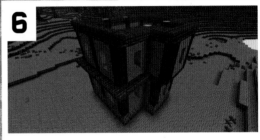

## 6

## LAYER

Put a row of wood on top of the walls. Line the sides of the building with stair blocks on top of each row of wooden blocks.

## 7

## FRAME

Make a frame for the ends of the roof in a stair shape out of wood blocks. Use the same pattern for the smaller roof above the entrance and then add the chimney.

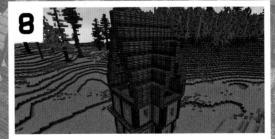

## 8

## FILL

Use jungle wood to fill the gaps between the roof frame. It is easier to start with the largest roof segments.

## 9

### DETAIL

Fill the space in the roof segments with clay, leaving openings for windows. The detailing is made from wooden stairs that start at the centre of the roof segment.

## 10

### WINDOWS

Put glass panes into the window openings, and add window detailing using wooden slabs, stairs and fence parts. Add detailing to the base using cobblestone and cobblestone stairs. The wooden blocks on the roof segment could also be replaced with wooden stairs.

## 11

### ENTRANCE

Add wooden and cobblestone stairs leading to the entrance, and then place the door. Add a small porch roof made from fencing, wooden slabs and wooden stairs.

## 12

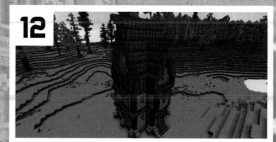

### FINISHING TOUCHES

Your finished house should look like this.

# MEGATON

**Server:** BlockWorks team server (private)
**Shaders:** Custom shaders for FalloutMC
**Mods:** WorldEdit, VoxelSniper
**Time to build:** Three weeks
**Blocks used:** 526,113

Inspired by a town of the same name from the game *Fallout 3*, Megaton is a fortified shanty settlement set in the wasteland of a post-apocalyptic Washington, DC. The town is built in the crater of a bomb explosion from scraps of metal and scavenged materials, giving it a run-down and dilapidated aesthetic. This is something that is very difficult to achieve in Minecraft®, but one of BlockWorks' leading builders, Rowanos, executed the project brilliantly, capturing perfectly the town's dark and gloomy atmosphere.

Perhaps the greatest challenge posed by Megaton was its size. Measuring only 150x115 blocks, the town is very small compared to the majority of other town/city projects. Many of Megaton's structures are made from disused industrial containers, old abandoned vehicles and other scrap items – the town's gate is fashioned from the wreckage of a crashed plane.

## THE BUILDER
Rowanos is a student from the Netherlands and one of the oldest members of the BlockWorks team. His experience is particularly apparent in his Megaton project, where he has taken the box-shaped voxels of Minecraft and transformed them into natural and organic shapes; at a glance you might not realise this project was built in Minecraft. Rowanos also has a talent for building at the smallest scales, carefully using slabs, stairs and tiny components to produce builds that are compact yet incredibly clean and precise.

# BUILDING REMAINS

While neat and complete buildings can be a challenge to create, ruins and remains can be particularly difficult, as building with square blocks doesn't lend itself easily to chaotic structures.

## BASE AND FRAME
Start by creating a base and frame for your wall section. Bombed structures don't have even edges, so layer your blocks so that all the edges are crooked.

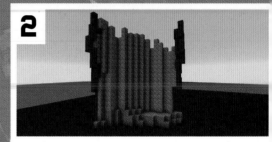

## FILL
Fill in the wall by building in different-sized columns, giving the wall an uneven surface.

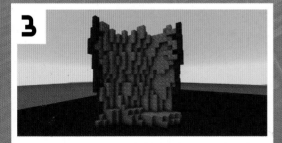

## TEXTURE
Punch out blocks to give your wall an even more rugged texture.

## DETAIL
Create some holes to suggest decay and use different materials to show varying degrees of deterioration.

**5**

# FINISHING TOUCHES

Finish your wall with a natural material to suggest moss or plant growth; ladders can be used for vines.

# SHANTY SALOON

This tutorial explains the construction method for one of the structures in Megaton: the saloon. To give the building its dilapidated finish, the structure is comprised of stacked boxes, which are then brought together with a number of continuous details.

## 1

## FRAME
Create the frame by making square and rectangular outlines in different materials. Use wood, metal and other materials that suggest scavenged items. Stack the boxes together in the general shape of a shack.

## 2

## WALLS
Fill in the box outlines with various different materials. You can use any blocks you like, but stick to drab and muted colors, such as grey and brown. The idea is to create a 'patchwork' effect of scrap metals.

## 3

## ROOF
Build up your roof with layers of slabs and various metal-like materials. You want to create an uneven surface.

## 4

## DETAILS
Add cyberpunk details such as vertical copper piping and a security peep hole to achieve a dystopian look.

## 5

### LAYER
Place a final layer of slabs and scrap materials to complete the fragmented structure of the saloon.

## 6

### SIGNAGE
Lastly create signage for your saloon. Build a sloping sign out of wood on the roof. Choose a different grey material for each letter and spell out the name of your bar on the sign.

# OCTALYPTICUM

Octalypticum was inspired by the game *SimCity 5: Cities of Tomorrow*. The Octalypticum has a fully functional terminal, a senate and a variety of other futuristic features. The entire disk-like structure floats on water. It uses large water pumps and features an agricultural centre. These details of how the city functions are just as important as how it looks.

### THE BUILDER

Christian S. Nielsen is 21 years old and from Denmark. He is taking a year off from his education after leaving school. His hobbies are graffiti, stencilling, photography and playing Minecraft®. The Octalypticum is a one-man project. Christian wanted to make something ultra-futuristic as it's one of the more unusual styles of building not often used in Minecraft.

# CHRISTIAN'S TIPS

Test your ideas, working from photographs of real builds.

Measure the size of buildings by constructing the foundation first.

Build, build and build some more. If you notice a mistake in the construction, you can always change it, but just keep building!

# FUTURISTIC HOUSE

While futuristic cities and their buildings can appear very minimalist, they must still be reasonably functional and their purpose should be easily recognisable. As this type of city's style is very uniform, the houses in it can be copied over and over again, with just small changes made to their gardens to give them some individuality.

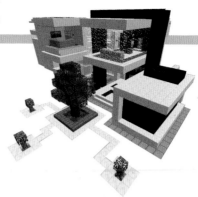

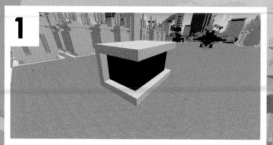

## 1

### BASE
Start by building a simple shape that's easy to change, move or rebuild.

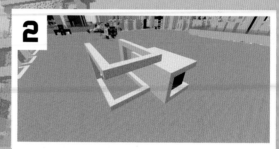

## 2

### MATERIALS AND STYLE
Build your house in keeping with the materials and architectural style of your city.

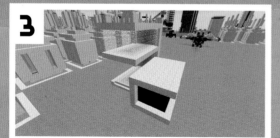

## 3

### FUNCTION
Consider the building's main function and decide now if you want to change it.

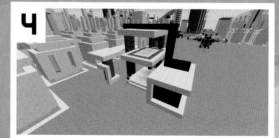

## 4

### DECORATE
Decorate the house with different colours or different types of blocks.

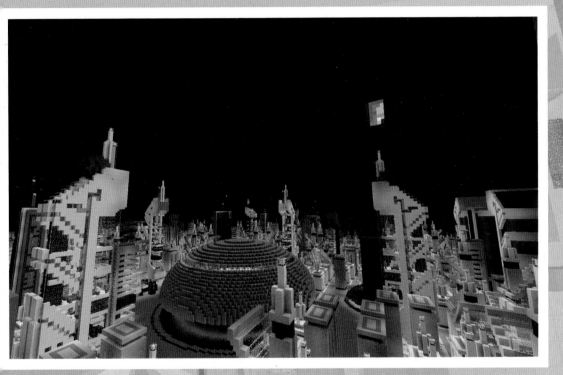

# FEATURES

Add some windows and interesting features once the basic shape is done.

# FURNISH

Add furniture and a garden.

# FUTURISTIC SKYSCRAPER

Tall, narrow buildings look great in a futuristic city. They have a sleek look that can be grouped together in districts to suggest a world removed from Earth, with humanity reaching for the skies.

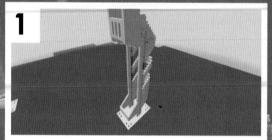

## 1

### SKELETON
Start larger buildings by creating a skeleton first, using plain blocks to make a special futurist shape. Leave holes where you want to place the windows.

## 2

### WINDOWS
Add glass in between the spaces you left for your windows when creating the skeleton.

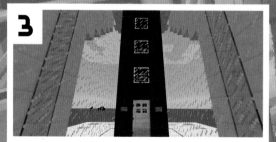

## 3

### FUNCTIONS
Move on to your interior construction. Start by defining where the lift is going to be.

## 4

### INTERIORS
Add different rooms and furnish them. You can use stair blocks as chairs and fences with pressure plates as tables.

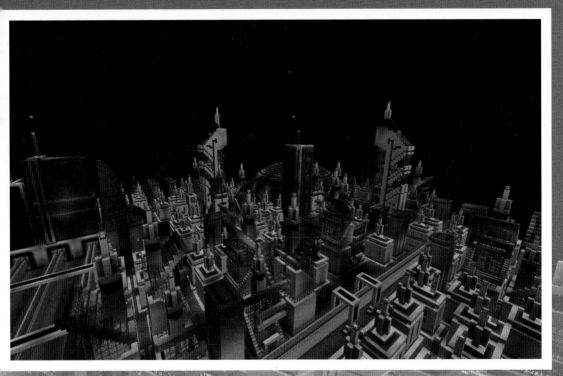

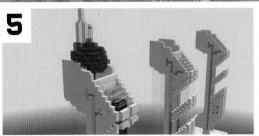

## ROOF

Add details to the roof area by adding trees, electricity pylons or antennas made out of fences or cobblestone fences.

## LIGHTING

Give the building lots of glowing blocks so you can see it at night as well.

# SYMPHONY: SKY CITY OF TOMORROW

**Blocks used:** White wool, quartz, stone slabs, blue stained glass, light blue stained glass, white stained glass, glowstone
**Time to build:** 15 hours

Symphony: Sky City of Tomorrow was designed as an entry to the Planet Minecraft website contest 'Head into the Clouds Project'. As part of the contest, a map with custom-made terrain was created for Symphony by Lentebriesje of the Angel Block Society. Builder Foxy used this as the basis for his sky city.

The style used for the build was inspired by the rigidness of neo-modernist architecture, combined with the fluidity and light-based elements of futuristic styles. Previous cities created by Foxy had inconsistent floor and street levels for a realistic look. However, he decided a perfect utopia would have more of an even, tiered progression of street heights, rather than a random hilly environment. This design decision gives the city its clean, organised appearance. The biggest challenge was creating the first level of the city.

### THE BUILDER
Foxy is an 18-year-old student at the University of Tennessee in Knoxville. He has always been fascinated by sci-fi concepts, such as self-sustaining utopias, spaceships, space exploration and colonisation. These ideas always had a bright, sleek, clean style.

As a big LEGO® fan, Foxy was quickly hooked when he started playing Minecraft. He began his building career creating futuristic spaceships, quickly attracting the attention of other Minecrafters and becoming part of a large community of spaceship builders.

He became increasingly interested in futuristic architecture and started building terrestrial complexes and cities in this style. Unlike most Minecraft groups, Foxy's community members rarely build or design together. Instead, they support and drive one another to develop unique styles.

# FOXY'S TIPS

Plot your concept on graph paper before attempting to build it in-game.

Observe a wide variety of sources and styles beyond the theme of your own design. Look for interesting elements and techniques that you can incorporate to improve your own builds.

Chances are your first attempt won't look like a masterpiece. Learn from failure. Go over your builds and see what you could do better next time.

# HOLOGRAPHIC SIGNAGE

Modern cities have a wide variety of services and machines available to the public, such as vending machines, directional signs, water fountains, street lights and so on. A futuristic city would likely have at least a few services that either don't currently exist or aren't very common – this tutorial is for the holographic information boards found in Symphony.

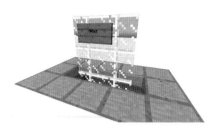

The edges are made of single stone slabs and the board is made of glass panes. Because single slabs don't connect to glass panes as normal blocks do, the boards will appear as floating sheets of glass. The flowing water and lights that will be placed under the board give the impression that some sort of energy is constantly running to and from the board.

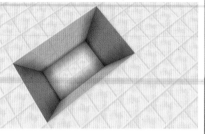

## 1
## HOLE
Clear out a hole that is four blocks deep, five blocks long and three blocks wide. The actual board will be two blocks shorter than the length of your hole (so here it will be three blocks wide).

## 2
## REDSTONE AND GLOWSTONE
Cover the bottom layer of the hole with blocks of redstone, then cover this with a layer of glowstone lamps (the sign has to be readable at night as well).

## 3
## WATER
Dig out a line of blocks in the longer side of the hole and fill the line with water so that it flows out onto the glowstone lamps.

## 4
## STONE SLABS
Go around the edges of the hole with single stone slabs. Make sure to use single slabs, as double-stacked slabs will not work for the next step.

## 5

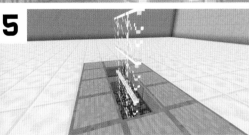

### GLASS

Make a wall of glass panes three blocks high starting from the level of the stone slabs. The panes should be directly above the water rather than in it.

## 6

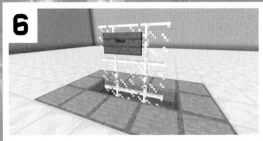

### BOARD

Customise the board however you want with signs, maps, paintings, item frames or other interesting elements you can think of.

**189**

# FUTURISTIC BUILDING

Designing buildings similar to the ones in Symphony is much easier than you might think. These structures are versatile in purpose and function, so you can always fit them into a city somewhere.

The colour scheme consists of a faded or simple base colour, a solid or metallic secondary colour and a bright, deep or neon colour for trim. The best blocks to use are ones that don't have a distinct border around the edges.

Materials such as quartz can make walls appear blocky and should be used for flooring. Wools work nicely for building walls, as they have a less defined beginning and end. Textures on walls of wool blocks blend together, giving the appearance of a single solid structure.

## 1
## CHEQUERED GROUND
Create a chequered ground of 3x3 squares in a flat world. (Programs like MCEdit are very helpful for processes like this.) You will be filling in each square according to what you draw in the next steps.

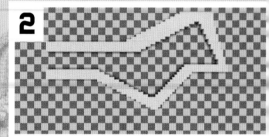

## 2
## FRAME
Sketch out a long overall frame of one of the side walls of the structure on the chequered ground you have made, which acts like graph paper. Aim to only use lines with slopes up to four blocks.

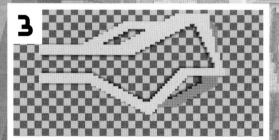

## 3
## SUPPORT BEAMS
Draw out some support beams and building extensions. These will be made of the blocks you chose for your secondary colour.

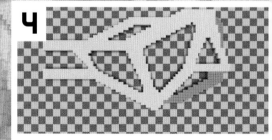

## 4
## CONNECTION BEAMS
Connect the long halves of the wall multiple times. These are your connection beams.

## 5

### FRONT WALL

Choose which direction will be the front and draw a rectangle the same height as the building sides. Draw lines crossing the rectangle at every height the slope of the side changes to guide yourself.

## 6

### BACK WALL

Create a back wall in the same way that you created a front wall.

## 7

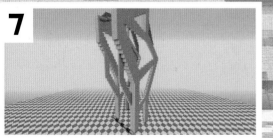

### STAND AND DUPLICATE

Now, either create a vertical grid or use a program like MCEdit to stand the wall up and make a copy of the wall at the distance you decided the length of the front and the back would be.

## 8

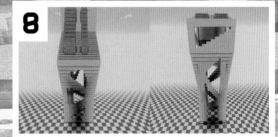

### ASSEMBLE

Stand the front wall and position it in front of the two standing side walls. Use it as a guide to filling in the front of the building. Repeat the same process for the back wall.

## 9

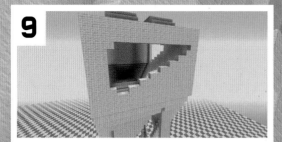

### TIDY

Now that you've built the frame, you can clean it up a bit. Slightly round out the areas in the frame where your windows will be going, so they appear more organic.

## 10

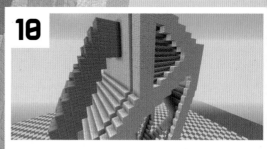

### DETAIL

Add a few extra details of your own. For this particular build, the smaller top windowpane was filled with glowstone behind stone slabs, instead of stained glass.

## 11

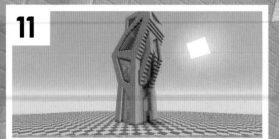

### WINDOW PANES

Build one space behind the panes rather than putting glass directly onto the frame. First go around the pane once with blue stained glass, then once with light blue glass, and then fill the remainder with white glass.

## 12

### FLOORING

Finish the building by changing the ground floor to quartz and adding floors of quartz too. Build a water lift from the top down the centre of the building and fill the floors with whatever you want.

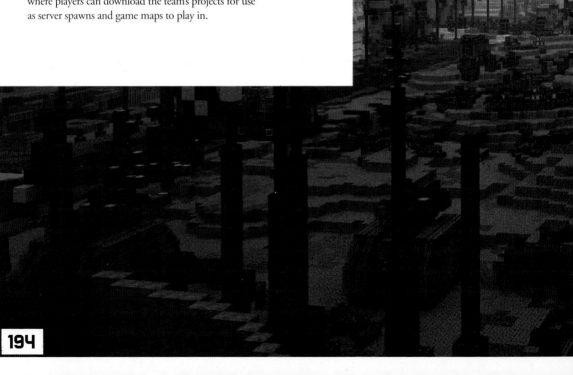

# WASHINGTON, DC

**Server:** BlockWorks team server (private)
**Shaders:** Custom shaders for FalloutMC
**Mods:** WorldEdit, VoxelSniper
**Time to build:** Ongoing
**Blocks used:** One billion+

Inspired by the post-apocalyptic video game, *Fallout 3*, this build is a full replica of the city of Washington, DC, reimagined after a nuclear holocaust. The iconic structures of Washington's centre – the Lincoln and Washington Memorials, the Capitol building and the Smithsonian museum – are all replicated to scale, with the National Mall transformed into a mass of trenches, shelters and fortifications. This project was particularly time-consuming, as the method of construction was to build the structures in full before wrecking parts of the buildings to give them an authentic worn and dilapidated appearance.

## THE BUILDERS

BlockWorks takes the idea of a Minecraft building team to a professional level. They collaborate with different groups around the work, take commissions and are able to work to deadlines, creating some of their builds very quickly, despite their huge scope and high level of detail. BlockWorks has its own store on their website, where players can download the team's projects for use as server spawns and game maps to play in.

# BLOCKWORKS' TIPS

Inspiration from other video games and movies can be a great starting point for your build, but you'll still have to use your imagination and ingenuity if you want to create a fully realised city.

It's important to be consistent with the sort of blocks used in an atmospherically moody build such as this one.

# CHAPTER 4

# HISTORICAL REALMS

# AMPHIPOLIS

The creators of Amphipolis have a passion for history, and this build was inspired by the rich and romantic architecture of the ancient Greeks. With the aim of creating an immersive historical experience in Minecraft®, the two leaders of building group Origines set out to construct Amphipolis.

The city features a Greek acropolis, a palace that incorporates the styles of the ancient Myceneans, an agora of municipal buildings and market stalls, and the many homes of the city's residents, ranging from the poor to the incredibly wealthy. Players can stroll the streets and view the grand monuments, opulent homes or run-down slums made up of ruins and hovels. Once the sights have been taken in, a bustling harbour and an island of quarries, caves and old temples lie outside the city walls.

The city of Amphipolis not only includes an impressive rendition of ancient life, but also an open world full of settled areas and natural wonders to complement the city. The creators take pride in allowing players to pass outside the city limits and explore other features that were a part of ancient Greek life and necessary for survival in an ancient city. Additional credit goes to Lentebriesje, for creating a number of trees featured throughout the island.

### THE BUILDERS

Amphipolis was created in partnership by two builders: 17-year-old Philip Wilkinson from San Francisco, California, and 21-year-old archaeology student Jeroen Bennink from the Netherlands.

Philip has a strong passion for ancient history and art and bringing antiquity to life through digital media. The two met through Minecraft servers focused on Roman culture and have been working together ever since.

Jeroen hopes that in the future he can combine his expanding knowledge of archaeology and passion for history with exciting new technologies to bring these fascinating ancient cultures to the masses.

**Shaders:** Sonic Ether's
Unbelievable Shaders
**Mods:** WorldEdit
**Time to build:** One month

**Point of interest:** The city is best viewed
with the Romecraft or Conquest resource
packs. The server, Respublica, plans on
releasing a combination of the two soon.

HISTORICAL REALMS

# GREEK TOMB

The ancient Greeks valued their ancestors greatly and set out to construct impressive mausoleums and tombs for them when they died. Such tombs were also the perfect place to commemorate their heroes – men of valour and bravery.

This build is for an ancient Greek grave, but it can also form the basis of a more complex mausoleum. It is best to use blocks such as sandstone or quartz, with flowerpots to represent urns and vases; these pots can stand alone or can be placed on brick blocks.

If you expand this tutorial, you could easily construct a large graveyard to honour heroes worthy of myth and legend. An ambitious builder might even take on the task of reconstructing the Mausoleum at Halicarnassus.

## 1 FOUNDATION
Start by laying a 4x4 foundation where you can place the chest or coffin. Sprinkle sand blocks around to create a small sand path.

## 2 SURROUND
Completely surround the chest with blocks so that it is hidden from the sides and finish one side with stair blocks.

## 3 ORNAMENTATION
Place two ornamental blocks on top of the chest, then add upside-down stairs at both sides.

## 4 DECORATE
Use flowerpots and brick blocks to make vases. Scatter some pots around. You can add pressure plates on top of the tomb for some extra detail.

**5**

## FINISHING TOUCHES
Adding tall grass will break up the flat shape of the ground and create aesthetic interest.

# PHILIP'S TIPS

When creating a large ancient Greek city, it is best to start by constructing its most important area – the district containing the city's temples. From there, you can radiate outwards and construct the city's other buildings. Once all of the structures are complete, the city's fortifications can be built.

Greece does not have an entirely flat landscape, and neither do most of its cities. It's important to work with terrain and not alter its original form to great lengths when constructing the city. When buildings flow with the landscape, individual structures typically appear more interesting and unique.

It's impossible to research all the buildings that existed in ancient Greece. However, you can apply structural features seen on one building to others. A temple's columns can be used elsewhere – in a rich man's house or roofed marketplace, for example.

# GREEK SHRINE

A small shrine to honour the gods will typically draw upon the structural style of a Greek temple, such as the Parthenon in Athens. However, it is important to note that a shrine is far less grandiose, as it serves to provide a place of worship rather than personal and communal prestige. Sandstone and quartz materials dominate this shrine, but wood is included due to the structure's humble origins. In some cases, wood can be the primary material used. Pots are usually a necessity, as priests would have to store vital materials to conduct complex rituals. The ideal spot for a shrine varies: it might appear in a rural ancient Greek village, or it could be situated within an acropolis worthy of the gods' respect.

### 1

### FOUNDATION
Lay the foundation of the shrine by setting down a 7x7 square in the ground, with a smaller 3x3 square at its centre.

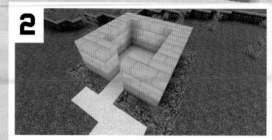

### 2

### WALL
Erect a two-block-high wall on the inner ring of the outer foundation, leaving space for a door.

### 3

### FINISH BASE
Add an outer ring of wall and place stairs around the top.

### 4

### WALL
Add a four-block-high wall to the inner ring using ornamental blocks around the entrance.

## 5

### LAYER

Add wooden slabs to the upper half of the fourth block, all the way around the structure. Build upside-down 'T' shapes on top of the front and back walls of the shrine.

## 6

### ROOF

Use brick slabs to build an elegant roof overhang by placing a slab on the upper half of the highest brick. Work down until you reach the wooden slab border.

## 7

### LAYER

Connect the two ends and fill the gaps by adding more brick slabs.

## 8

### DECORATE

Place a couple of vases around the structure and some lone flowerpots to represent offerings for the gods.

## 9

### PLACEMENT

Position your shrine in a suitable setting. It could be located by the tomb from the previous tutorial, as a place of worship for hero cults.

# THE BABEL CITY

Sharing the epic proportions of its biblical namesake, this project features a monumental palace set against the background of a tropical mountainous region. The influences of Arabic and Eastern architecture can be seen in Babel's minarets and domes, while the sandstone textures also suggest a structure of Eastern origin. Despite its size, this project succeeds in maintaining a high quality of detail throughout – the overall effect of which is stunning.

## THE BUILDER

GroovyMoose is a Norwegian student and one of the most experienced members of the Minecraft® building community. Known for his epic-scale structures and high-level detailing, he has played a key role in many of the large BlockWorks group projects and is a vital member of the BlockWorks community. He hopes to pursue his creative interests as an architect.

**Server:** BlockWorks team server 2
(private)
**Shaders:** Sonic Ether's
Unbelievable Shaders

**Mods:** WorldEdit, VoxelSniper
**Time to build:** Four weeks
**Blocks used:** 7,845,402

HISTORICAL REALMS

# BLOCKWORKS' TIPS

When adding detail to a build, be careful not to add too much. Over-detailing a project can often make it difficult for any features of the build to stand out. Using balanced amounts of detail will enable you to draw attention to specific areas of interest.

Classically styled builds often use symmetry, but it is useful to offset that symmetry with some more irregular features. Terrain should never appear symmetrical – repetition or patterns will make it unrealistic and artificial looking.

While you are building a structure, try to consider its interior at the same time. By focusing solely on an exterior, you are likely to make the task of creating an interior far more difficult. The exterior and interior of any project should be planned concurrently.

# BEIJING CITY 1751

Known as Project 1845, this build is a 1:1 scale replica of Beijing City in China, as it appeared in 1751. It is based on the oldest complete map of Beijing, which was made during the reign of Emperor Qianlong. Once completed, the model aims to break the world record for the largest historical scale replica built in a game.

Starting with a blueprint and reference material about Chinese architecture, the team started building in July 2011 with the lofty ambition of re-creating every unique structure as accurately as possible. The team has also included a population of non-playable characters to simulate trade flowing through the city. This brings visitors into a realistic historical environment that provides a personal connection to the culture, history and identity of the city.

With every house, room and garden being custom built, the project is expected to take 10 years to complete. The biggest challenge is accuracy: if something is measured inaccurately it can lead to knock-on problems that have caught the team out several times.

### THE BUILDERS

Taylor 'Bohtauri' Cook is a 28-year-old New Zealander who is working on Project 1845 full time. Bohtauri began Project 1845 three years ago while living in Beijing, China. The build is a non-profit educational project that aims to encourage history education in a virtual setting. In this way, the city will teach people about history from a first-person perspective, unlike anything seen before.

More than 200 volunteers, ranging from 14 to 60 years of age and from all around the world, have helped build Beijing City, bringing new tools to schools to teach students in an engaging way.

**Server:** project1845.net
**Shaders:** Sonic Ether's
Unbelievable Shaders

**Mods:** WorldEdit, VoxelModPack
**Time to build:** Three years (so far)
**Blocks used:** 137 million to date

HISTORICAL REALMS

# FORESTED PARK

In the 18th century, Beijing City had a lot of farmland and forested parks. It is quite a challenge making trees accurately and to scale, while also making them aesthetically pleasing, but this tutorial will help you create an entire forested park.

## TREES
Build five of each type of tree, ranging from three to five blocks away from the central trunk. This is the most time-consuming step and should be done carefully and slowly. The rest is easy!

## GRAVEL
After you have mapped your park, use WorldEdit to select a one-block layer that is well above your park. If you want a random scattered effect of trees, replace this layer with 0.2–2% gravel and let the gravel drop (a dense forest has about 3–5% density of trees).

## PASTE
At each gravel block, paste in a random tree from the set of trees you built in step 1.

## COMPLETE
Enjoy your custom forested parkland. With its randomly placed trees, the forest will not appear too uniform or look like it has simply been copied and pasted.

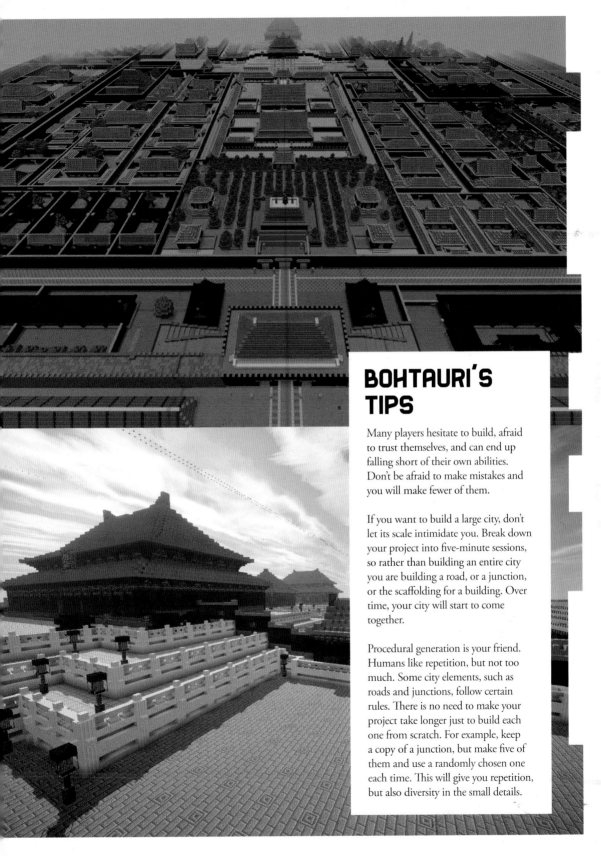

# BOHTAURI'S TIPS

Many players hesitate to build, afraid to trust themselves, and can end up falling short of their own abilities. Don't be afraid to make mistakes and you will make fewer of them.

If you want to build a large city, don't let its scale intimidate you. Break down your project into five-minute sessions, so rather than building an entire city you are building a road, or a junction, or the scaffolding for a building. Over time, your city will start to come together.

Procedural generation is your friend. Humans like repetition, but not too much. Some city elements, such as roads and junctions, follow certain rules. There is no need to make your project take longer just to build each one from scratch. For example, keep a copy of a junction, but make five of them and use a randomly chosen one each time. This will give you repetition, but also diversity in the small details.

# IMPERIAL ROOF

Minecraft® is not very curve friendly. Because of this, many players are afraid to try Asian architecture, but it is certainly possible to make a structure that is aesthetically accurate while keeping to scale. There are a lot of styles that are considered Chinese – this one is in the style of an imperial roof from Northeast China during the Ming Dynasty.

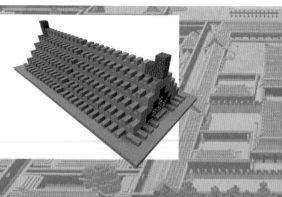

## 1

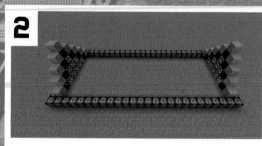

### OUTLINE
Make sure your roof outlines have an uneven number of blocks for their width. This is to ensure that the top of the roof is only one block wide. If you need them to be even in number, line the top with two rows of stairs facing each other.

## 2

### SIDE WALLS
Build the side walls of the roof one block in from the outline. Most imperial roofing is golden, with a liberal use of gold and red decoration.

## 3

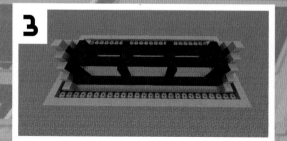

### RAFTERS
Build the internal rafters. Vertical beams need enough space between them for three rooms.

## 4

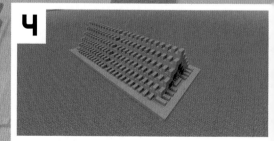

### ROOFTOP
Build yellow blocks across the top of the rafters, then place stair blocks as shown. This gives the appearance of the roof tiles that help water flow down. In the middle it should appear as an extra wide groove.

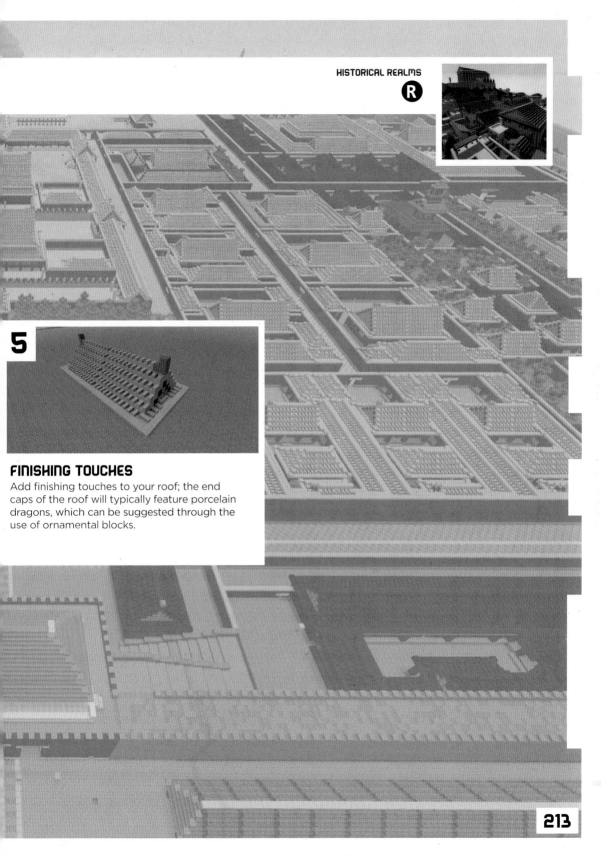

# 5

## FINISHING TOUCHES

Add finishing touches to your roof; the end caps of the roof will typically feature porcelain dragons, which can be suggested through the use of ornamental blocks.

# CHERNOBYL 2015

Chernobyl 2015 was designed as an arena map after Adam was inspired by the documentary film *Alone in the Zone* by Arkadiusz Podniesiński.

The Jakpok Cooperative has always shared an interest in the abandoned city of Prypiat, and Poland has many Soviet-style buildings, which made it easy for the Jakpok Cooperative team to re-create the recognisable landmarks in the zone – the Ferris wheel, 'Lazurnyj' swimming pool and Duga-3 Radar are all visible. The Chernobyl power plant itself was too big to fit into the boundaries of the map, so only the infamous reactor number 4 was re-created.

To make the environment more foreboding, the map's biome was set to desert and swamp to remove all the bright colours, and a texture pack with a gritty, post-apocalyptic look was used. To make combat more interesting, canals were added below the city, as was an underground base with a half-sunken boat in the harbour. Radiation warning signs and portraits of Lenin were added as custom textures, and all of the signs were written in Russian (by team member Igor, who speaks Russian fluently).

### THE BUILDERS
The Jakpok Cooperative is a Polish team of three school students, Jakub 'Jakpok' Pokorski, Adam 'Haddock' Kawecki and Igor 'Niko' Jasik, who are interested in creating adventure maps, survival games, PVP Arenas and mini-games in Minecraft® using a variety of unusual themes.

**Shaders:** Sonic Ether's
Unbelievable Shaders and custom
resource pack

**Point of interest:** There are interesting
lettering marks in Polish in the abandoned
Summer Camp in the Chernobyl map. These were
copied from Adam's school desk!

HISTORICAL REALMS

# IKARUS BUS

Ikarus was a brand of bus used in Soviet states. It is said that during the evacuation of Chernobyl and Prypiat the government used more than 900 Ikarus buses to evacuate more than 60,000 people. The buses were so radioactive that they were subsequently abandoned in the contamination zone.

## CHASSIS
Use black wool to make wheels and connect both axles with stone slabs.

## LAYER
Put a single layer of red stained clay on top of the chassis, with the exception of the central block at the front.

## WINDOWS
Install the front window and add side windows every second block. Add a window in the centre at the rear of the bus and remember to leave some space for front doors. Use a dispenser or furnace as a front grille.

## FILL
Use iron blocks or another smooth, metallic material to fill the gaps between the windows. Install iron doors at the front.

# JAKPOK'S TIPS

Use some buildings and trees as stencils to copy and paste around the map.

Almost all post-Soviet countries have similar architecture – if you know it, you can easily re-create Eastern landscapes.

Remove colours that detract from the look of the landscape.

## 5

### LAYER

Fit a couple of nether brick stairs inside the body, matching them to the windows. Add a single layer of stone slabs on the top.

## 6

### FINISHING TOUCHES

Use stone buttons as rims in the wheels and also as front and rear lights. Use levers to imitate side mirrors and an exhaust at the rear.

# IMPERIAL CITY

Imperial City started as a 19th-century city. This allowed a variety of styles because much of the architecture of the period was based on the revival of older styles. As the city expanded, the team started to organise the buildings, with many changing several times. It also began to look at other sources of inspiration, adding gothic, renaissance, steampunk and fantasy elements to the city. As a result, the city has been overhauled several times, with half of it built on a central island between the two arms of a river and the rest built on the banks.

The incremental building process has added realism to Imperial City. Just as a real city is like a living being that constantly evolves, the accumulation of various styles and the constant changes made by the team have had a similar effect. As the construction has advanced, more details have been added to the structures and more attention paid to the interiors.

The team members' underlying ambition was always to improve their individual skills and impress viewers with a city that seemed real at first sight. Although the city has been built almost exclusively by two brothers, they have welcomed help from a few builders in France, Britain, Belgium and Spain late on in the project.

## THE BUILDERS

Imperial City was created by two French brothers, one a cardiologist in France, the other a banker in Chile. As big fans of architecture, history and design they quickly decided to use their server to start work on a large city with impressive monuments that would challenge the technical limits of Minecraft®.

Their style is always realistic, with a focus on buildings that appear credible and are designed with the laws of physics in mind. They particularly like styles from the 18th to early-20th centuries, typical of old cities such as Paris, Vienna, London, Berlin, Saint Petersburg, Chicago and New York.

**Time to build:** Two years (so far)
**Blocks used:** Approx. 1,250 million (2500x2000x250)

**Point of interest:** The largest and highest build is the Winter Palace, based on the Palace of Justice in Brussels, at 200 blocks long and 256 blocks high.

# SPHINX STATUE

Given the size of the blocks, building statues is always a challenge in Minecraft®. One option is to create a very large structure, which makes it possible to include curves and suggest movement, but to keep things simple, here is a quick way to represent a reclining sphinx (or lion) using just four blocks!

## 1

## FRONT LEGS

Select plain blocks and stairs of the same material; it can be wood, cobblestone or quartz. At the front, place a stair block to create the front legs.

## 2

## BACK LEGS

Add another stair block to represent the statue's back legs.

## 3

## BODY

Place a regular block between the stairs to represent the body of the animal.

## 4

## HEAD

On top of the front 'legs', add another stair block to represent the statue's head. You now have a small figure that can be used to decorate a building, a garden or the sides of a path.

# THE BROTHERS' TIPS

Think big! If you want to make realistic buildings, you need a high level of detail and the ability to represent small things. A large structure allows more-convincing details and realistic decorations such as statues and ornaments to produce facades with depth.

Making copies of existing builds is a good way to learn. It teaches you how to make well-balanced structures and how to successfully express the codes of any given architectural style in the world of Minecraft®.

Share your builds, play with others and learn from them. This can be fun and stimulate your creativity to a point you could never predict. The brothers behind Imperial City had no particular skills in building when they started – they are not architects, engineers or artists, yet their skills improved dramatically.

# ANCIENT TEMPLE

This Greek temple should take about an hour to build if you follow the instructions. For extra help, you can watch the creator build the temple on his YouTube channel, The French Whisperer.

## 1

## FOUNDATION
Build a cobblestone pedestal to raise the height of the building. The dimensions used here are 24x18x3. Add cobblestone stairs to provide access to the pedestal.

## 2

## COLUMNS
Add quartz columns around the pedestal, with a two-block gap between each one. You can use stairs at the bottom of the columns and on top (inverted) to give them a Grecian look. Replace one quartz block at the bottom and top of each column with a decorative block.

## 3

## WALLS
Within the perimeter surrounded by columns, raise walls of the same height. Use cobblestone for the ridges and quartz for the filling of the walls. Make an entrance in front of the stairs.

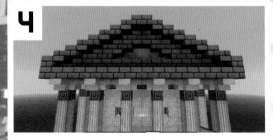

## 4

## PEDIMENT
Build a triangular cobblestone pediment, two to three blocks thick, on top of the columns at each side of the temple. Dig into the pediment to give it a sense of depth.

## 5

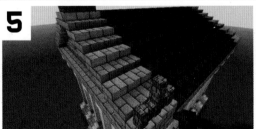

### DECORATE
Join the two triangular pediments with blocks of a contrasting colour, such as nether brick or wood. Add little decorations on top and at each side of the pediments.

## 6

### INTERIOR
You can arrange the interior to suit your taste, perhaps replacing blocks from the pedestal with wool to make a carpet, building a small altar in the back of the temple or placing torches here and there for the lighting.

# LEM CATHEDRAL

The Lem Cathedral project was originally developed by Bill Silverlight, founder of the build team LanguageCraft. The inspiration for the build was Durham Cathedral, in England, but a whole team later transformed the project into a city. Centred around the cathedral, a bank, barracks, market and trading port began to appear.

One of the most difficult aspects of the build was to convey the medieval feeling of houses placed close together with narrow streets between them. It was a great learning experience for the team, which needed to develop a style and find new ways for players to feel immersed in a city. The build helped to mould LanguageCraft's speciality – atmosphere.

After the project was finished, it emerged again as a collaboration between LanguageCraft and Team Eventime. Over the course of eight livestreams, both teams redid the terraforming and built the huge castle that you can see in the background.

### THE BUILDERS
The medieval city of Lem was LanguageCraft's first real team project. The build was led by Bill Silverlight, Dedelush and Micromega, who shaped LanguageCraft's style and ideals, especially in the early days when the trio did most of the building.

In the real world, Dedelush is David Renoux, a 22-year-old Frenchman who works in landscaping. Big is never big enough for Dedelush, and he won't be content until he has reproduced all of the historical monuments in Paris, France.

Micromega (Pierre Ecrepont) was in his final year of high school when he worked on Lem. Now age 20, Pierre has attended architecture school, dabbled in archaeology and currently works in botany.

**Server:** LanguageCraft
**Mods:** WorldEdit, VoxelSniper,
OptiFine and Camera Studio

**Resource pack:** Dokucraft Light
**Time to build:** 300 hours
**YouTube channel:** youtube.com/LanguageCraftTV

**HISTORICAL REALMS**

R

# MARKET STALL

The market can take you on a journey to a world of commerce and social contact, especially in an urban environment. In Lem, it marks the transition between different zones and breaks the monotony of roofs, while reinforcing the rustic feel.

A single stall isn't enough for a market – four or five is a good number for a build of this size. Historical context is also important. In a medieval city, stalls in the street are much more common than the covered markets you might find in an Arabian setting. The same goes for materials, and wood and wool will be your main blocks. To convey the right atmosphere, try to set the stalls in a disorderly fashion and use different coloured wool for each one.

## 1 FOUNDATION

Locate your stall in a busy street, close to a main square where people get together. Place wooden beams as foundation.

## 2 FLOORING AND SIDES

If you are building a permanent stall, add some kind of ground or flooring. Raise wooden fences to support the canopy, as well as gates where people go in and out.

## 3 CANOPY

Wool is a must for your canopy and for any fabric in Minecraft®. For smaller stalls, you can go with carpets on fences; stripes are recommended, alternating two colours.

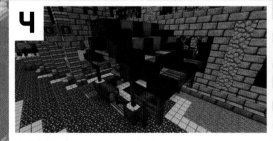

## 4 DETAIL

For more detail, add another canopy made of wooden slabs to one side, with fences acting as an articulating support. You can add trapdoors on the sides too, for hanging storage.

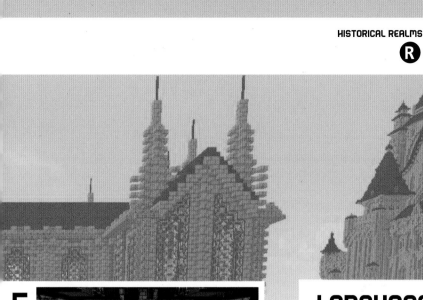

# 5

## DECORATE

Add small decorations. This will make or break your market's atmosphere and can suggest what each stall is selling.

# LANGUAGECRAFT'S TIPS

Roofs are one of the hardest and most time-consuming parts of a build, so you should think about them as soon as you start. In the case of medieval buildings, it is much easier to make a pointed roof if a building's width is odd numbered.

To add details to your build, you can use items that don't take up a full block, such as slabs or stairs. Buttons and trapdoors can also be used to make patterns or add detail.

# MEDIEVAL HOUSE

Houses are the central element of an urban setting. This tutorial will help you build a peculiar timbered house that leans on existing houses and is built over the main road and a secondary path. To present a homogenous feeling, houses must be grouped together and have the same general characteristics – that's how you determine the different neighbourhoods in a city.

The actual timbers are hard to represent, because in reality wooden beams are not so wide. However, building in Minecraft® is all about cheating and finding tricks to work around these difficulties. Use planks, logs, cobblestone, stone and glass as the main materials – other materials will also be used here and there.

## LAYOUT
Start by marking your house's layout. Buildings are often stuck together in medieval cities, so you need to know where you are building to so you don't run out of space.

## FIRST LEVEL
This is the first part of your house. It needs to feel solid. Use materials such as stone and stone brick for the first level.

## BEAMS
Use wooden beams to structure your house. Don't forget about where you want to place windows when you set up your vertical beams.

## WALLS
Fill in the walls behind the beams with stone and add windows. You should allow the beams to stick out for relief.

## 5

## DETAILS
Add details to your facades with fences. Build a lip for your roof that will go around the top floor of your house.

## 6

## TILING
Lay the tiling on your house. Go from bottom to top, and then change materials in a second pass to break the evenness.

## 7

## ROOF DETAIL
Add a couple of dormers along the roof, as well as a chimney – the aim is to break up any flat surfaces.

## 8

## FINISHING TOUCHES
Finish the roof by working on its edges. Vary the shapes by using stairs and slabs, or perhaps even anvils. Get creative!

# PROSPERO CANAL CITY

The inspiration behind Prospero Canal City was large townhouses in European cities. The properties are close together and very tall, so they take up less space. Parisian houses were used to generate ideas, with some elements taken from late 17th-century German castles and incorporated into the build.

Lead designer, Cjrainbolt, liked the houses so much that he decided to make a whole city from them and challenged himself to fill it with canals. The city features a huge cathedral on a hill, an early-20th-century battleship, a train station with a giant dome, a giant castle and a plethora of houses, bridges and boats.

The main issue with building Prospero was time – Cjrainbolt had just one month to build this four-million-square-block city, and with school finishing at the same time, exams had to take precedence!

### THE BUILDERS

Cjrainbolt is TheReawakens team's head designer, and he initiated the Prospero build with the help of the team. TheReawakens started out on a small server in Denmark and grew to become a large international team. The team plans to become one of the most creative in the Minecraft® community, inventing magical and inspiring builds. Their philosophy is to make every day a happy one when playing and to help one another achieve their aims.

**Server:** TheReawakens
**Shaders:** Sonic Ether's
Unbelievable Shaders

**Mods:** Camera Studio
**Time to build:** One month
**Blocks used:** Four billion

# AIRSHIP

Airships are a good way to test your skills. Get creative with all the materials you have and make your airship fit your build. In this tutorial, the balloon uses stained clay to make it appear old. For the body, wood looks good on this design, and a tail on the airship gives it a steampunk vibe.

## 1

### BALLOON

Make a long, flat balloon out of stained clay. This one measures 15 blocks long, five blocks wide and five blocks tall. The clay gives the balloon a rough look.

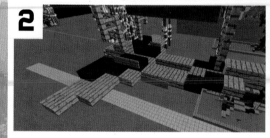

## 2

### CART

Build a cart underneath the balloon, using a mix of dark and oak wood slabs. Connect it to the balloon with wooden fences. Add wings to the back of the cart.

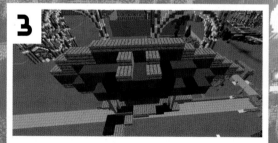

## 3

### LAYER

At the top of the balloon, add a layer of wooden slabs from the front to the back, extending them a little way under the balloon as well.

## 4

### TAIL WINGS

At the back of the balloon, add a tail made from a mix of wooden slabs and wooden fences. Fences should be inside the tail wing and stick out in front of the wing.

# THE- REAWAKENS' TIPS

A good plan can take longer to design than the city takes to build.

Make templates of your buildings, such as houses, farms and castles. You can use these designs to fill out your city.

Never leave a surface plain. If there is flat surface around add blocks and make a pattern to give it some detail.

# BALLISTA

When building in a medieval style, you need big weapons that fit the theme. Siege weapons are ideal to complete a fortress. This ballista is just one example, but there are lots of ancient siege weapons you could attempt. No castle would be complete without a trebuchet or battle ram threatening from outside the gates!

## 1

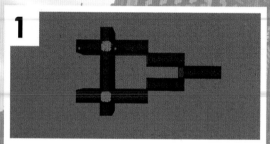

### FRAME
Lay out your frame. Be sure that you make each log the correct size. It should be three blocks long at the back and two blocks long at the front.

## 2

### EXTEND
Extend the back with two blocks, each rising one block. At the front, build two blocks up, then squeeze in to the middle and add two three-block pillars.

## 3

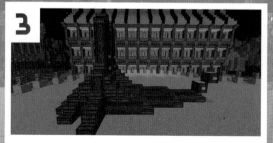

### LAYER
Put wooden stairs on the frame at the end of all the logs. For the uprising frame, add wooden stairs as support.

## 4

### RAMP
Add a ramp from the top of the uprising frame to the back of the ballista. Let it fall half a block each step down. Make a hole at the top for the arrow.

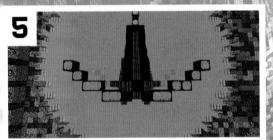

## 5

## BOW

On top of the uprising frame add the bow. Suspend it from the centre using the following order on each side: 3, 2, 1 and 1 blocks.

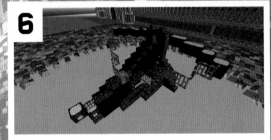

## 6

## CHAIN

At the back of the bow, add a chain. Suspend it from the bow ends, running back to an iron block at the centre. From that block it should run straight back to the end of the ballista.

## 7

## COBBLE FENCE

At the front of the bow, add cobble fence below and in front of it. Support the cobble wall with stairs underneath.

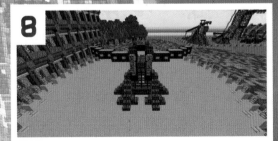

## 8

## FINISHING TOUCHES

Add buttons to the front of the bow. Experiment with ladders on the bare surfaces of the wooden logs for a finishing touch.

# VITRUVIAN CITY

Vitruvian City features a number of cathedrals, palaces and other city structures and houses, mostly in a Renaissance style. It also features perfectly sculpted landscape gardens, although its main feature is a replica of Cologne Cathedral.

The city is named after the philosopher Vitruvius and Leonardo da Vinci's famous drawing 'Vitruvian Man'. The idea of proportion was important for both.

### THE BUILDER
Dariusz Dubiniec is a 38-year-old security officer from Swiebodzin, Poland, now living in Nottingham, England. Dariusz has a passion for historical Western architecture, with a particular interest in gothic, Renaissance and baroque cathedrals and palaces, which he researches thoroughly before incorporating them into his builds.

**Point of interest:** Features a replica of Cologne Cathedral, which in real life took more than 600 years to build, but Dariusz re-created it in a fortnight in Minecraft®.

HISTORICAL REALMS

# DARIUSZ'S TIPS

While perfect symmetry can make a build appear less realistic, it is very useful for landscape gardens. Creating a template flowerbed and then copying it can create an excellent replica of grand palace gardens.

When creating a replica of an existing building, it's important to understand the history of the architecture and the architect to really master the building. Historic builds are a great way to learn about the culture and history of the world. Take the time to find out how the buildings you are re-creating were used.

# TERRAN'SYL

Terran'Syl was built as a set for Creative Community, a French team responsible for the Minecraft® web series *Starcube Galaxy*. Precise layouts had to be made before work began to make certain that both LanguageCraft and Creative Community would be happy with the result in terms of its aesthetics and suitability to the script.

The city is Arabic/Persian in design, with a different feel for each neighbourhood. The market has very narrow streets and roofs dotted with bricks, while the poor neighbourhood around it is labyrinthine, with houses straddling each other. At the opposite end of the spectrum, the wealthy neighbourhoods have wide streets and greenery. This is also where the city's monuments can be found.

Terran'Syl marks a turning point in the LanguageCraft team's history, as this is where the team really started to work on relief patterns on walls several blocks thick, which has become a hallmark of their builds.

### THE BUILDERS
Terran'Syl was an early project led by LanguageCraft's founder, Bill Silverlight (in real life, Matthew Thornton, a 24-year-old French-American, YouTuber, actor and award-winning director).

Passionate about video, Matthew launched his YouTube channel in August 2011 and over time has rallied a large team of builders, graphic artists, developers, moderators and writers. He is now one of the most well-known Minecraft YouTubers in the French-speaking community, and he strives to spread the love of building to as many people as possible through his speciality – timelapses and cinematics.

Let's Timelapse, one of Matthew's most successful series, bridges the gap between Let's Play videos and timelapses of builds. The videos serve to teach history as well, using historically accurate builds. Matthew is also the creator of the award-winning short film *Minecraft: More Than Just a Game*.

**Server**: LanguageCraft
**Shaders**: Custom mix of Sonic Ether's
Unbelievable Shaders and Chocapic13's Shaders
**Mods**: WorldEdit, VoxelSniper, OptiFine, Camera
Studio and Custom NPC
**Time to build**: Three weeks
**YouTube channel**: youtube.com/LanguageCraftTV

**HISTORICAL REALMS**
**F**

# PALM TREE

It might not seem necessary to build custom trees in Minecraft®, but they enable you to make your city more personal and emphasise the atmosphere a lot better than Minecraft-generated trees can. This tutorial is going to build a palm tree, but the various wood and leaf types in Minecraft mean that you can build any sort of tree, depending on the style of your project. You can also find libraries of trees online or make your own (as LanguageCraft has done) to be reused if it suits a new project. Start by finding a real-life model to imitate.

## 1

### BASE
This palm tree is relatively low, but its base still needs to appear solid. Stop the different trunks at different heights to make it look more natural.

## 2

### TRUNK
Move the trunk away from the base to create a natural curve. WorldEdit enables you to change your trunk so that only bark is visible on all sides. A simple command makes your tree look much more realistic.

## 3

### LEAVES
Don't hesitate to use an image as reference to make the most realistic shape possible. Depending on the type of tree, you can fluff up the leaves or vary the type you use.

## 4

### FINISHING TOUCHES
Small details will help make your tree more convincing. Be creative by using items such as fences, vines and melons. In this example we are adding a cocoa bean.

# LANGUAGECRAFT'S TIPS

If you switch between many different styles with each project, as LanguageCraft does, it is important to always use the best tool for the job. That means always choosing the most appropriate resource pack. It will help you dive into the new style and help with immersion.

For a detailed build, it is important to make walls that are several blocks thick (two at the very least, four is ideal). This gives your building depth and relief and allows you to have elements jut out, such as a window ledge, or have them carved into the wall.

Try to make patterns by using different materials, such as stairs and slabs. You can repeat them along your building to give it unity, but try to find the right balance. Variety is important – a facade that is repetitive is also boring.

# PERSIAN HOUSE

Houses are the basic building found in any city, especially simple houses where most of the population lives. In this case, however, a wealthy house will be tackled, as it offers more of a challenge. If you can manage this type of house, then building basic houses shouldn't be a problem.

Keep in mind that 'perfect' buildings are boring: they don't exist in real life and are too linear. That is why we will be placing blocks on the facade in a seemingly random manner, to give the construction a broken-down feel.

This is especially important for roofs, which are huge surfaces – don't hesitate to break blocks here and there. Sandstone is a great material for this, as it gives access to stairs and slabs of the same material.

## 1

### FOUNDATION
Try to imagine the shape you want for your structure by drawing out its base. This will help you to visualise how much space is available for the interior.

## 2

### MATERIALS
Choose all the blocks to use on a build before starting. This will help you to identify colour schemes and prevent bad mixes.

## 3

### LEVELS
Set up the posts and flooring of all the floors of the building. Be sure to leave at least three blocks between each floor, as it is a wealthy house.

## 4

### WALLS
Fill in the walls in a flat manner with the material that will serve as the canvas. In this instance, sandstone is used to convey solidity.

## 5

### LAYER

Build up the wall using different materials. Items that don't take up a whole block are your best allies, but beware of repetition.

## 6

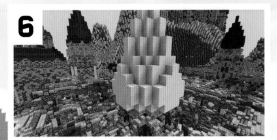

### TURRET

Create an oval shape with a pointed end, as shown above, to sit atop a turret for your house.

## 7

### ROOF

Flat roofs are difficult to make, as you need to occupy the space to stop it from looking too boring. This building will have a roof garden at one side, while the remainder will be patterned using stairs.

## 8

### ROOF DETAIL

Have the roof spill over the edge using stone brick slabs for a better contrast.

## 9

### FINISHING TOUCHES

As a finishing touch, add vegetation, tables, ponds, vines – all those elements that make a structure truly alive.

# CONTRIBUTOR DIRECTORY

## ADAMANTIS
Jamdelaney1
Team: Blockworks
Web: http://blockworksmc.com
YouTube: https://www.youtube.
com/user/BlockWorksYT

## AETERNIUM
Team: Blockworks
Web: http://blockworksmc.com
YouTube: https://www.youtube.
com/user/BlockWorksYT

## AMPHIPOLIS
Philip Wilkinson and Jeroen
Bennink
Twitter: @Origines_Leon

## ANDROMEDA
Team: Blockworks
Web: http://blockworksmc.com
YouTube: https://www.youtube.
com/user/BlockWorksYT

## APPLE'S INFINITE LOOP
## HEADQUARTERS, CUPERTINO
Michael Steeber
Web: http://michaelsteeber.com

## ATROPOS
MinerArchitect (Carlos)
YouTube: https://www.youtube.
com/user/MinerArchitect

## THE BABEL CITY
GroovyMoose
Team: Blockworks
Web: http://blockworksmc.com
YouTube: https://www.youtube.
com/user/BlockWorksYT

## BEIJING FORBIDDEN CITY
Bohtauri Taylor (Taylor Cook)
Team: Project 1845
Twitter: @Bohtauri
Web: http://project1845.com
YouTube: https://www.youtube.
com/user/BohtauriTaylor
Server: project1845.net:65525

## CHERNOBYL 2015
Jakpok (Jakub Pokorski),
Haddock (Adam Kawecki),
with Niko (Igor Jasik)
Team: Jakpok Cooperative
Youtube: https://www.youtube.
com/user/JakpokCo

## CHICKEN COVE
YukiYupi (Yuki Lin) and
Citronizer (Reijo Wong)
Server IP: 108.166.172.51

## CLOUDHAVEN
Dan Lynch
Team: Angel Block Society

## THE DESERT CITY OF ALAMUT
Anairrh (Luke Dargatz)
Youtube: https://www.youtube.
com/user/anarrih

## EMPIREPOLIS
CzechPower1 (František Hanzlík)
with Bmilez (Blair Miles)
Facebook: https://www.fb.me/
Empirepolis?fref=ts%20-

## FORGEHEART
Sanaken Soryu (Tobias Wolfbeiß)
Team: Sanacraft
Twitter: @SanacraftMc

Web: http://sanacraft.enjin.com
Server: sanacraft.mcfrag.
net:25665
Server IP: 185.16.84.72:25665

**GREENFIELD CITY**
Oskar Sutton
Twitter: @OskarSutton
Facebook: https://www.facebook.
com/GreenfieldCityMinecraft
Server: greenfieldmc.com

**HUNTINGTON CITY**
Yazur Strovoz (Joey Girard),
MancoMtz (Raul Martinez),
GhostrXzz, and AlphaRebel
Team: Esterlon
Twitter: @YazurX
Web: http://yazur.deviantart.
com
YouTube: https://www.youtube.
com/user/AlphacraftTeam
Server: http://esterlon.enjin.
com/home

**IMPERIAL CITY**
Comeon and Rigolo
YouTube: https://www.youtube.
com/user/Rigolo0

**LAPIZ POINT**
Yazur Strovoz (Joey Girard),
MancoMtz (Raul Martinez),
GhostrXzz, and AlphaRebel
Team: Esterlon
Twitter: @YazurX
Web: http://yazur.deviantart.com
Youtube: https://www.youtube.
com/user/AlphacraftTeam
Server: http://esterlon.enjin.
com/home

**LEM CATHEDRAL**
Bill Silverlight (Matthew
Thornton), Dedelush (David
Renoux), and Micromega (Pierre
Ecrepont)
Team: LanguageCraft
Twitter: @LanguageCraft
Web: http://languagecraft.tv
YouTube: https://www.youtube.
com/user/LanguageCraftTV

**MATTUPOLIS**
Matius Buks
Website: http://mattupolis.
blogspot.fi
YouTube: https://www.youtube.
com/user/Mattupolis

**MEGATON**
Rowanos
Team: Blockworks
Web: http://blockworksmc.com
YouTube: https://www.youtube.
com/user/BlockWorksYT

**OBSIDIAN CASTLE**
Michael Newton
YouTube: https://www.youtube.
com/user/TheLegendNewton

**OCTALYPTICUM**
Christian S. Nielsen

**PIRATE ISLAND**
Heaven Lord

**PROJECT ZEARTH**
Xoyjaz (Yashar Irandoust)
Web: http://xoyjaz.tumblr.com
YouTube: https://www.youtube.
com/user/Xoyjaz/

## PROSPERO CANAL CITY
Cjrainbolt
Team: TheReawakens
Twitter: @TheReawakens
Web: http://www.reawakens.net
YouTube: https://www.youtube.
com/user/thereawakens
Server: Play.reawakens.net

## PYRAMID ADVENTURE
Jakpok (Jakub Pokorski),
Haddock (Adam Kawecki),
with Niko (Igor Jasik)
Team: Jakpok Cooperative
YouTube: https://www.youtube.
com/user/JakpokCo

## REDLIGHT CITY
Golonka Swe
Web: http://golonkaswe.tumblr.
com/
YouTube: https://www.youtube.
com/user/underage117

## SIMBURBIA
Jigarbov (Tim Gehrig) and
rsmalec (Ron Smalec)
Youtube: https://www.youtube.
com/user/jigarbov
YouTube: http://www.youtube.
com/rsmalec

## SYMPHONY: SKY CITY OF TOMORROW
Foxy

## TWIN PEAK SKI RESORT
Daniel Thage and Cjrainbolt
Team: TheReawakens
Twitter: @TheReawakens
Web: http://www.reawakens.net
YouTube: https://www.youtube.

com/user/thereawakens
Server: Play.reawakens.net

## THE VILLAGE - ADVENTURE
## MULTIPLEX 2
Jigarbov (Tim Gehrig)
and rsmalec (Ron Smalec)
YouTube: https://www.youtube.
com/user/jigarbov
YouTube: http://www.youtube.
com/rsmalec

## VITRUVIAN CITY
RezolutnyDarek
(Dariusz Dubiniec)
Web: http://www.
planetminecraft.com/project/
vitruvian-city

## VORPAL CITY
Salmon77 (Joshua Haun)
YouTube: https://www.youtube.
com/user/salmon771

## WASHINGTON, DC
Team: Blockworks
Web: http://blockworksmc.com
YouTube: https://www.youtube.
com/user/BlockWorksYT

## YATHERIN PALACE
Daniel Thage
Team: TheReawakens
Twitter: @TheReawakens
Web: http://www.reawakens.net
YouTube: https://www.youtube.
com/user/thereawakens
Server: Play.reawakens.net

# PICTURE CREDITS

# INDEX

# GALLERY

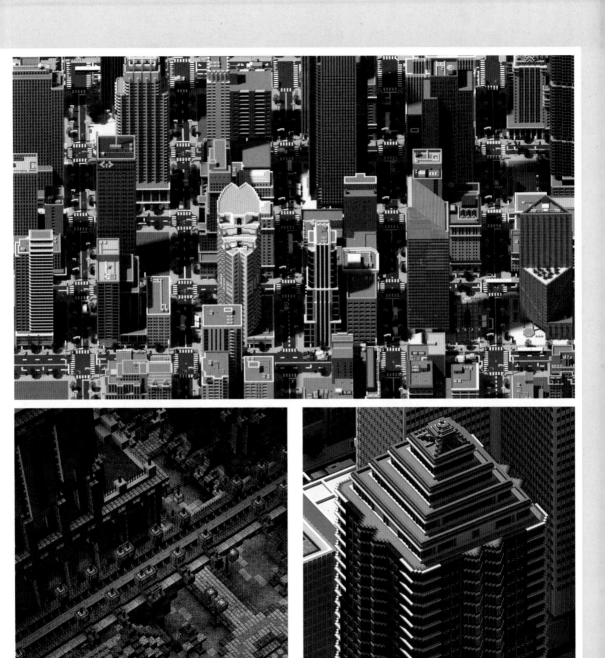

# ABOUT THE AUTHOR

KIRSTEN KEARNEY is a games journalist who began her career at the BBC. She is the author of an eBook for Gameleon on freelance games journalism and was section editor for *Guinness World Records: Gamer's Edition* for two years. Kirsten runs www.ready-up.net, which has been nominated for a Games Media Award for four years running. She has given radio interviews on Minecraft® and runs a children's Minecraft server.

*With*

YAZUR STROVOZ (Joey Girard) is founder of the public server Esterlon. Yazur and his team of contributors are the builders behind Huntington City and Lapiz Point, two of the most realistic and detailed cities in Minecraft.

# ACKNOWLEDGEMENTS

For Max and Dan.
Thanks to the Kearneys, Crawfords, Smiths and McNivens.
Thank you Linda for listening. Special thanks to Ellie, Leon, Tanya, Lorraine and Peter. You know why.

— Kirsten Kearney